THE SPACE BETWEEN HER LEGS

Tiffany Antone

BROADWAY PLAY PUBLISHING INC
New York
www.broadwayplaypublishing.com
info@broadwayplaypublishing.com

THE SPACE BETWEEN HER LEGS
© Copyright 2023 Tiffany Antone

Cover art: Tiffany Antone

First edition: November 2023
I S B N: 978-0-88145-989-0

Book design: Marie Donovan
Page make-up: Adobe InDesign
Typeface: Palatino

CHARACTERS & SETTING

MAYBELL, *her vagina leads to space*
CHOW, *Chinese American, attitudilicious*
JIM, *a dude's dude*
GYNA, *a socially awkward gynecologist (pronounced like Gina)*
PETE, *an astrophysicist*
VINCENT, *JIM's roommate*

The Space Dudes:
JARED
NICOLÁS
LEON
ELI
BEN
KUMAIL

Ensemble Players: (doubling encouraged)
DETECTIVE 1 *(male)*
DETECTIVE 2 *(male)*
NURSE
GYNA'S DATE *(male)*
BARISTA
GHAZAL
COFFEE HOUSE PATRONS
JUDGE JENKINS *(male)*
THE CLERK
MAXINE SHARP (MAYBELL's *lawyer*)
DISTRICT ATTORNEY BUCHANAN *(male)*
US ATTORNEY EICHMAN *(male)*

AGENT BUNCH, *CIA (male)*
AGENT X, *FBI (male)*
GENERAL AIELLO *(male)*
EPA CHIEF *(male)*
NERVOUS SCIENTIST *(male)*
SCIENTIST 1
SCIENTIST 2
SCIENTIST 3
BUTLER

Time: Now

*Locations: There are quite a few locations in this piece—
thus, locations can be suggested with minimal set pieces and
furniture.*

*On Acting in Space: Yes, it would be grand if you had an
anti-gravity bubble for the actors to play in, but in lieu of
that, please have fun figuring out how to put the dudes in
space!*

*Cast: This is an ensemble play, and there are several different
roles to be split amongst your company. Please cast the net
wide and include a diverse range of peoples in this play.*

ACT ONE

Prologue

(MAYBELL's *apartment*)

(*Er, more specifically,* MAYBELL's *[admittedly messy] bedroom.*)

(MAYBELL *and* JIM—*a hottie from the club—are banging it out in her bed. It's clumsy and maybe a little weird, but they're finding their groove…*)

(*Or, more accurately,* JIM *is finding* MAYBELL's *groove.*)

(*He's finding her groove reallll good…*)

MAYBELL: OhmygodOHmyGOD-OHMYGOD! YES! YES! YES!

(*Maybe too good…*MAYBELL *is climaxing and, well, the fabric of space and time literally TEAR apart when she does.*)

(*What.*)

(*The.*)

(*Fuck?*)

(JIM *is blinded by the…what is it? Is that a…a motherfucking quasar? Did a giant motherfucking wormhole open up to reveal a motherfucking QUASAR emanating from between this woman's legs?*)

(*Yes.*)

(*Yes it fucking did.*)

JIM: What the shit?

(MAYBELL *is still yodeling like she's the only climber on the mountain, while the wormhole between her legs begins to collapse inward...pulling a very freaked out* JIM *along with it!*)

(*A cosmic "Whooosh!" ripples across the sheets as* JIM *disappears after the quasar.*)

(MAYBELL *lies spent...still...is she...?*)

(*"SNORE"*)

(*Yep. That bitch is asleep.*)

Where There's Smoke...

(MAYBELL*'s apartment*)

(MAYBELL *and her bestie-from-another-nestie,* CHOW, *are discussing the mysteries of the universe over wine, weed, and snacks.*)

(*A pair of men's pants sit nearby.*)

(*Every once in a while, a strange beep pipes in.*)

CHOW: I don't understand why you just don't bang at their place.

MAYBELL: Because I can't pee at a dude's apartment, and you know how prone I am to UTIs—

CHOW: Oh, yeah, holding it in is a major do-not!

MAYBELL: Right, but my bladder goes on lock-down if a guy's around. I can't stand the thought of some hottie McHot-Ass hearing me take a piss—

CHOW: You don't think they'll hear you here? These walls are whisper thin.

MAYBELL: I pee in my sink.

CHOW: The fuck did you just say?

MAYBELL: I, stop staring at me! It makes sense—

CHOW: No, Maybell, it does not.

MAYBELL: Just, listen—I hate the pee-hitting-the-water sound going in a toilet makes, so when a guy's here, I just go in the sink instead—

CHOW: Holy tofu-fucking-Christmas!

MAYBELL: Shut up! It doesn't make any noise that way!

CHOW: The sink I just washed my face in?

MAYBELL: Yes, but I clean it—

CHOW: How often?

(MAYBELL *shrugs…*)

MAYBELL: Often.

CHOW: Did you clean it before I got here? Maybell? Tell me you scrubbed that sink with bleach before I put my poor, caring, unsuspecting best-friend-face in it thirty fucking minutes ago, or so help me—

MAYBELL: Yes. Yes, of course I scrubbed it before you came over. Jeez.

(Beep)

CHOW: Thank you. Now I can breathe easier knowing I don't have to scrape my face off because it came in contact with your coochie-water. Jesus. Maybell, that's the most disgusting thing I've ever heard!

MAYBELL: No it isn't.

CHOW: It is. And I've got four brothers.

MAYBELL: Whatever.

CHOW: No, that's some seriously fucked up truth you just spilt! And—I'm saying this as a friend—but I think maybe you need help, like, *professional* help, about this whole pee-in-the-sink thing—

MAYBELL: Thanks.

CHOW: —BUT, you're still like, the sweetest person I know. You're TOO sweet. I mean, if you were any nicer to the assholes you bring back here, they'd die.

MAYBELL: Yeah, right.

CHOW: Seriously. They'd curl up, balls-up, from your love poison. It would just be stiffs with stiffies around here for as far as the eye could see.

MAYBELL: Oh my God—

CHOW: You could pee wherever you wanted then. You could pee on their faces! Their cold, dead, sweetly-murdered faces—

MAYBELL: OH MY GOD!

CHOW: AND, you could steal their wallets.

MAYBELL: Now we're talking.

CHOW: No one would blame you. "Asshole death-spiral-itus" from boffing-and-offing on the sweetest woman alive!

MAYBELL: I'm not the sweetest woman alive.

CHOW: You're sweet enough.

MAYBELL: Semi-sweet, maybe.

(A beep)

CHOW: That wouldn't be a bad super power, though. Saccharine sex poisoning? You could rent your services out to women whose husbands are cheating on them.

MAYBELL: Eww.

CHOW: You could have business cards made up— "Sweet Revenge". No phone number. Just a what-do-you-call-it—

MAYBELL: —I couldn't sleep with strangers for money—

CHOW: —Are you kidding? Between the pissed off wives and their husband's bulging wallets, you'd be so rich, you could pay for all the hoo-ha cleaning and "Please-God-help-me-to-stop-peeing-in-the-sink" therapy you need.

MAYBELL: I don't need therapy—

CHOW: A QR code! Is that still a thing?

MAYBELL: For like, your phone?

CHOW: Yeah. I don't know. It would take them to your secret website—

MAYBELL: Nothing is secret on the internet.

CHOW: You could use the dark web.

MAYBELL: What the fuck is that?

CHOW: It's what money launderers and mob guys and human traffickers use—

MAYBELL: Jesus!

CHOW: It's so fucked up.

MAYBELL: Fucked!

CHOW: But if you were to open a sex assassin business, that's totally where you'd need to operate.

MAYBELL: Chow, this is dumb.

CHOW: Whatever. Pass me the nut bowl.

MAYBELL: Are you eating the cashews?

CHOW: Yes. You're so weird. Who doesn't like cashews.

MAYBELL: Me. Listen, I can't kill men with my sweetness. It just repels them. And I don't want to kill them, even if they do ditch me faster then…an elephant with diarrhea

CHOW: Gross.

(A beep)

MAYBELL: —I just want to do a better job of selecting sex partners in the first place. It's like I've got some kind of radar that says "Hey, dickheads! This one sleeps like a rock!"

CHOW: The radar thing is real. It's standard predator-prey stuff. They can also tell when we're ovulating. They don't know it, but they can. It's why, like, twenty-five percent of one-night stands result in pregnancy.

MAYBELL: That is not a real thing.

CHOW: I dunno, seems like everyone I know is pregnant right now, and most of them were totally caught off guard.

MAYBELL: Jamie said Frank knew before she did.

CHOW: What? How is that possible?

MAYBELL: He said her vag tasted like pineapple.

CHOW: He is so full of shit.

MAYBELL: That's what he said.

CHOW: No one's vag tastes like pineapple.

MAYBELL: Yeah, exactly. So he knew something was up when hers starting tasting like pineapple.

CHOW: Stop saying "Pineapple!" Jesus, I'm hungry. *(She grabs more nuts.)* Listen, the point is, if these fuck-bunnies keep ditching you, and you still haven't found one who'll stay around by the time you're like, thirty-five, you could stop popping that pill and start gambling. I'd be the best auntie ever—

MAYBELL: OMG, I'm SO not even thinking about babies right now.

(A beep)

CHOW: What the SHIT is that sound?!

MAYBELL: I don't know, but listen—I'm not stuffing my face right now with you because I'm mortally depressed that I can't find someone to marry and start popping out kids with. I'm stuffing my face because the only thing men seem to like about me is my "Hey, I'm easy!" mating call and it's pissing me the fuck off!

CHOW: That is not your only asset. Also, you've slept with like, half the guys I've slept with. So who's easy now?

MAYBELL: They always hit and run, though. Every. Single. Time. Even the guys I make wait, Chow. Leon and I had four-point-five dates before I let him into bed with me, and he left so fast, he didn't even remember to take his coat!

(Beep)

MAYBELL: I have a whole box full of abandoned menswear in my closet!

CHOW: That. Is. SO. Fucking. Annoying.

MAYBELL: It's insane!

CHOW: No, I mean the beep. I want to find it and murder it!

MAYBELL: It's probably the, you know, the goddamn fire-detector batteries or whatever. Can you pass me the cheese?

(CHOW does.)

CHOW: Hey, you should come with me this weekend.

MAYBELL: Silent yoga? No way.

CHOW: It's better than the fire alarm nagging you—

MAYBELL: I can't sit in silence for three days! I'll go crazy. Do you have any idea how much neurosis is locked up in here?

CHOW: That's my point.

MAYBELL: I don't want to unlock it, Chow. It will take way too long to put away again once I'm done.

CHOW: There's a purging ceremony—this isn't just a yoga retreat, it's a mindfulness and women's strength thing too.

MAYBELL: I'll have to sit still, drink vegetable broth... chant. I can't handle that—

CHOW: Your sexual walk-about isn't working.

MAYBELL: I'm doing research.

CHOW: Mhm. And what have you learned?

MAYBELL: Engineers are just as rowdy as aging frat boys, the banker was allergic to my cat, and Jim—

CHOW: That's last night?

MAYBELL: Yeah. Jim was sooooo...athletic. I had a hard time keeping up. I was so tired that I don't even remember if I O-ed or not. I gotta stop smoking this shit and get my ass to the gym.

CHOW: Wait, you don't remember climaxing?

MAYBELL: Well, I probably did. You know I have that, weird, fall-asleep-after-I-climax thing—

CHOW: When you come home and rub one out by yourself, yeah, I remember. But I just chalked that up to you always starting out with a couple glasses of wine first. You're telling me you *always* fall asleep after an orgasm?! Like you have, what, sexo-lepsy, or something? Are you a narco-sexual?

MAYBELL: I sleep the sleep of the dead. It's deeply restorative—

CHOW: Coitus-Inter-Nap-tus. Jesus, Maybell, there's your answer.

MAYBELL: What do you mean?

CHOW: You don't make sure these guys yodel before you pass out on them—

MAYBELL: Mountain climbing analogy. Nice.

CHOW: Thank you.

(Beep)

CHOW: —OH MY GOD, where the fuck is your fire-alarm thing?

MAYBELL: In the hall?

CHOW: It's driving me crazy! *(She heads to the hall…)*

MAYBELL: I don't think you can un-install it without setting it off—

CHOW: I'm going to knock it down and take out the battery.

MAYBELL: Okay.

CHOW: *(OS)* Listen, if you pass out on these guys before they get their rocks off, of course they're not sticking around.

(Beep. Clunk. Bang)

MAYBELL: Chow, he left his shoes and pants here! His SHOES and PANTS! It's so awful I "might" have passed out that he left and abandoned his *shoes and pants*? We could have had morning sex! I could have made it up to him. I don't know if he came or not—but his shoes and *pants*?

CHOW: *(OS)* That's weird.

MAYBELL: Fucking right, it's weird.

CHOW: *(OS)* No, "shoes and pants" has like, no meaning to me anymore. Shoes and pants, shoes and pants, shoes and pants… *(She enters with alarm, rips out the battery, throws both on the sofa.)*

CHOW: There. I'm hungry.

MAYBELL: We've been eating all night.

CHOW: I know. God, I need this weekend. No junk food. No drinking. No smoking. Just quiet.

MAYBELL: We could order something—

(A knock at the door.)

CHOW: Oh my God, what if that's Indian food!

MAYBELL: It's not Indian food.

CHOW: You don't know that.

MAYBELL: We haven't ordered anything yet. It's probably the Super, angry because you took down the fire alarm.

CHOW: Psh—

MAYBELL: Or it could be the mail-person with my Vibe-of-the-Month delivery—

CHOW: I keep forgetting to sign up for that!

MAYBELL: Chow, I get, like, two free vibrators if you use my coupon code.

CHOW: I'll do it, I'll do it. Geez.

(Knock. Knock)

MAYBELL: It could be Jim…

CHOW: He's hear for his shoes and pants!

MAYBELL: I'll tell him that I donated them—

CHOW: You ate them!

MAYBELL: My cat took a crap on them!

CHOW: Oh my GOD, that's perfect! Where's the cat-box?

MAYBELL: What?

CHOW: I'm totally rubbing this cock-hat's pants in some cat shit.

MAYBELL: Chow—

CHOW: Maybell.

MAYBELL: What if he's here to apologize?

CHOW: Then you can hand him back his cat-shit pants as a token of how not-accepting of his apology you are.

(CHOW *and* MAYBELL *tug of war with the pants.*)

MAYBELL: Give them to me!

CHOW: No way. You have to take a stand sometime, Bell!

(*Knock, knock, knock*)

(MAYBELL *loses the tug of war.*)

(CHOW *cackles as she runs off with the pants in search of the cat-box.*)

CHOW: God, I hope it's Indian food.

(MAYBELL *takes another hit, opens the door.*)

(*Two* DETECTIVES *stand outside.*)

(MAYBELL *does not know what to do with the pot smoke filling her lungs…so she holds her breath as long as she can…*)

DETECTIVE 1: Are you Maybell Marks?

(MAYBELL *nods.*)

DETECTIVE 1: Do you know a James Kling?

(MAYBELL *thinks, shakes her head.*)

DETECTIVE 2: Are you sure? He's been missing since last night.

(MAYBELL *makes a "I don't know any Jameses" face…*)

DETECTIVE 1: That's weird, because we've been pinging his cell-phone with our geo-tracker and it led us here.

(MAYBELL)

(MAYBELL's *confusion*)

(*The smoke in* MAYBELL's *lungs…*)

DETECTIVE 2: His roomate said he went home with an… (*Consults notes*) …"Okay looking chick" (*Looks up*) Is that you?

DETECTIVE 1: Sure looks like it could be.

DETECTIVE 2: Anyway, he hasn't been back since, hasn't answered his phone all day, and his roommate says that's totally unlike him because, and I quote, "Jim never bangs and hangs".

(MAYBELL's *eyes bulge.*)

MAYBELL: Jim?

(MAYBELL's *voice cracks as the smoke escapes in a hacking cough—right in the* DETECTIVES' *faces.*)

(*At the same time,* CHOW *emerges from the hallway with the now-fouled-pants held high.*)

CHOW: Thought you could fuck and run on my friend? Well, eat shit motha-fucker!

(*Beep*)

DETECTIVE 2: We call this probable cause.

Bad Cop…Bad Cop?

(*An interrogation room*)

(CHOW *sits at a table,* DETECTIVE 1 *and* DETECTIVE 2 *ask questions.*)

DETECTIVE 1: You call yourself Chow Li?

CHOW: That's my name, don't wear it out.

DETECTIVE 2: Says here your real name is Amber.

CHOW: Yeah, well, my parents were First Gen.

DETECTIVE 2: What?

DETECTIVE 1: —eration.

DETECTIVE 2: Oh. So?

CHOW: They wanted me to have an American sounding name.

DETECTIVE 2: Why pick Chow?

CHOW: I like it.

DETECTIVE 1: But you don't spell it Chinesey—

CHOW: Chinesey?

DETECTIVE 2: That's not- He's sorry. That's not appropriate. We don't know if she's Chinese or not—

CHOW: I'm Chinese-American.

DETECTIVE 1: So you should spell it with an "-ou" —not an "-ow".

DETECTIVE 2: You're an expert on Chinese names now?

DETECTIVE 1: I looked it up.

DETECTIVE 2: Whatever. You can't say to a Chinese person—

CHOW: Chinese-American.

DETECTIVE 1: She's using a pseudonym. It's suspicious.

CHOW: It's my name.

DETECTIVE 2: Not according to your driver's license.

CHOW: It's the name I go by.

DETECTIVE 1: But *why*, is what I'm asking.

DETECTIVE 2: That's a better question—

DETECTIVE 1: Why call yourself Chow, with an "-ow"?

CHOW: Because I like to eat.

DETECTIVE 1: Chinese food?

DETECTIVE 2: Haha, is that—can I laugh at that?

CHOW: What the fuck is happening?

DETECTIVE 1: We're interrogating you.

CHOW: You're being a couple of dumb fucking nit-wits, is what you're—

DETECTIVE 2: Hostile witness.

DETECTIVE 1: Hostile *accomplice*.

DETECTIVE 2: Right.

CHOW: You can spell Chow a lot of ways, fucktard. And I'm not an accomplice to anything. But you can bet your ass I'm making mental notes of every goddamn racist thing coming out of your dumb ass mouth—

DETECTIVE 2: Extremely hostile.

(DETECTIVE 1 *leans in close.*)

DETECTIVE 1: Where is James Kling?

DETECTIVE 2: We know he was with your girlfriend last night.

CHOW: So now I'm a lesbian?

DETECTIVE 2: No, I meant in the friend sense—

DETECTIVE 1: Did you help her dismember his body?

CHOW: What? No—

DETECTIVE 1: Were you there when she hacked him into bits?

CHOW: No one hacked anyone into anything—

DETECTIVE 2: Where were you last night between nine and midnight?

CHOW: Out.

DETECTIVE 1: Did you happen to pick up any lye? Bleach? Sharp objects for cutting into flesh—

CHOW: —the fuck?

DETECTIVE 1: Where is Kling's body?

CHOW: I don't know!

DETECTIVE 1: I think you do!

CHOW: He left! He screwed my friend and left. Who knows what happened to him after that. Fucker probably found another hole to stick himself into—

DETECTIVE 2: Will you listen to the mouth on her?

DETECTIVE 1: Her *girlfriend's* just as bad.

CHOW: That's the second time—

DETECTIVE 1: "Fuck you," and "Fuck that" all over the place.

DETECTIVE 2: You might want to cool it on the girlfriend stuff—

DETECTIVE 1: You started it.

DETECTIVE 2: I wasn't using it in an antagonistic way—

CHOW: I feel antagonized.

DETECTIVE 1: You're the perp!

CHOW: You're a cock-hat!

DETECTIVE 2: Now, now—

DETECTIVE 1: No, let her insult me. *(To* CHOW*)* I'll throw you in jail so hard, you'll wake up next year.

CHOW: So now you're threatening me with physical violence?

DETECTIVE 1: That was hyperbole.

CHOW: *(Counting on her fingers)* "Chinesey", lesbian, "I'ma' throw you"—

DETECTIVE 2: You were the ones too stoned to know the difference between the police and delivery guy—

CHOW: The city's gonna hand me both your asses on a gold plated platter when this is over.

DETECTIVE 1: Even if you continue to play stupid about Kling, we've still got you and your girlfriend on the whole bong and weed thing—

CHOW: FOR THE LAST TIME, I DON'T KNOW ANYTHING ABOUT KLING!

DETECTIVE 2: We're not getting anywhere with this one.

CHOW: You two suck at this.

In Space, No One Can Hear You...

(JIM *floats in space.*)

(*He wears no pants.*)

JIM: Where the fuck am I? I mean, I know it looks like… but, I'm not an astronaut, you know? So there's no way I'm in fucking *space*! People can't survive in space, they can't breath in space without an astro-suit, or whatever. *I'm* not wearing a suit— (*He looks down.*) SHIT. Where the fuck are my pants? (*He holds onto his balls.*) Think…think. Shit. The last thing I remember is that I went home with that chick…her name was, ah-it's a month in the calendar. She was alright looking. She thought I was funny. I mean, I am funny. She was cool. We went back to her place. We were totally getting it on! She had some good weed at her place. I was so into her weed! Wait, shit. Was there something in that weed? (*He looks around.*) If that chick drugged me I'm gonna', like, kill her or something. I've never done hard drugs before! I play basketball sometimes and I'm on an intermural hockey league with my boss—I can't fuck around with my performance. I hardly ever even smoke pot! But it was Saturday night and I wasn't totally into…WHAT IS HER NAME?! And I didn't have to buy the weed for once. SHIT-SHIT! Am I tripping out here in space while she's like, passed out next to me and maybe I'm gonna be laying around her strange apartment for hours while my subconsious floats around wherever the fuck this is? *(He looks down.)* I don't see why I can't have pants here. It's cold. If this is a bad trip, I should at least have pants. Maybe I'm cold because she's hogging all the covers. *(He yells…)* HEY—PUT A BLANKET ON ME! *(Nothing happens.)* Okay, that's obviously not going to work. I'm cold here, probably because my body is cold there, but it feels like my body is here with me, so I am really going to have to concentrate if I'm going to get my mouth there to work… I can do this. I can figure this out. I just need to get my body to say "Blanket". Blanket blanket…

The Inspection

(MAYBELL is in stirrups, the usual paper-esque tarp over her legs. She is handcuffed to the table.)

(GYNA the gynocologist and a NURSE enter.)

GYNA: Hello, er— *(Looks at chart)* Maybell. Pretty name!

MAYBELL: Okay.

GYNA: I'm Dr Scott, and this is— *(Looks at NURSE)* What's your name again?

NURSE: Suzanne.

MAYBELL: She already—

GYNA: Yes, Suzanne. Sorry. We don't work together much. She's here full-time, but they only call me in when they have lady problems like you—

MAYBELL: Lady problems?

GYNA: Drugs, vaginas—you know where this is going.

MAYBELL: It was a tiny bit of weed, and I didn't smoke it through my vagina.

GYNA: That's good. Good. I mean, it would be like, some kind of YouTube worthy skill if you *could* smoke it like that, right? But I still have to make sure you didn't hide the rest of your stash up there in a fit of panic—

MAYBELL: Yeah, I already told them I don't have any more.

NURSE: That's what they all say.

MAYBELL: I'm sure they do but—

GYNA: They do all say that.

NURSE: But you find out the truth.

GYNA: That I do, Suzette, that I do.

NURSE: Suzanne.

GYNA: Right.

MAYBELL: This is bullshit.

GYNA: Suzanne is here to make sure protocol is followed and that nothing untoward takes place.

MAYBELL: This whole thing is untoward.

GYNA: Nice. Not many pot-heads are able to turn a four dollar word around like that.

MAYBELL: I'm not a pot-head.

NURSE: That's what they all say.

GYNA: They do. They really do. Also, thanks Suzanne. Never be alone with a lady's vagina, is my motto. I don't need any practice getting sued for malpractice, if you know what I'm saying.

(GYNA *leans over* MAYBELL, *who reads her name tag.*)

MAYBELL: (*Mispronouncing it*) Gyna? You're name is Gyna? Gyna the Gyno?

GYNA: It's pronounced Gee-na, thank you.

MAYBELL: Gee-sus.

GYNA: If you could just relax your legs a little…

(MAYBELL *does not want to relax anything.*)

MAYBELL: Don't I get to call my lawyer or something, before you go ahead with what is surely going to be a gross invasion of my privacy?

GYNA: Inviting your lawyer to see your lady bits would be the gross invasion. I'm a doctor. I'm also a woman. You're in good hands here.

MAYBELL: But—

GYNA: Listen, Maybell—the police think you're stuffed like a Thanksgiving turkey up there. Only instead of bread crumbs and cranberry sauce, it's marijuana and amphetamines they're picturing./

MAYBELL: /They know I don't have drugs up my cooch. They're just pissed because they can't find the guy I banged last night and are using you to intimidate me.

GYNA: /The sooner I issue the all-clear, the sooner you're out of here and back in your cold little cell, panties up, legs crossed, happy as a clam, no joke intended! (*Not missing a beat*) I don't see anything about a "bang" on here. You're saying you had sex last night? Did you use protection? Because I can give you some brochures on the pill, IUD, or—

MAYBELL: OH MY GOD, stop it! I don't want you scoping my goodies. I don't give my consent. There's nothing up there and I am NOT okay with you forcing yourself into my junk—

GYNA: I hear you, Maybell. I really do. And let me tell you that it brings me no pleasure, no pleasure at all, to get called in here on a Saturday night just to wand some druggie's nether regions, but we all gotta pay the piper, and I need to pay my bills. And really, you're the one who decided to ride the weed train, amiright? (Don't answer that, I might get called to testify.) Now, can you scoot down just a little to the end of the table—

MAYBELL: No.

GYNA: Maybell...

MAYBELL: *(Mispronouncing it again)* Gyna.

GYNA: Sueanne?

NURSE: Suzanne.

GYNA: Whatever.

(The NURSE steps towards MAYBELL in order to help hold her in position.)

MAYBELL: THIS IS BULLSHIT! You can't force me to spread my—this is an invasion of my privacy!

GYNA: If you wanted to keep your vagina private, you should have moved to a blue state.

(The NURSE has MAYBELL in position.)

GYNA: Okay, how's my hand temperature? Good?

MAYBELL: Seriously?

GYNA: Yes.

MAYBELL: It's fine.

GYNA: Awesome. Now—you're going to feel a slight pressure... And then, I'm just going to insert these two fingers...

(GYNA is silent, the NURSE watches.)

(GYNA removes her hand.)

GYNA: Initial physical examination shows nothing out of the ordinary.

MAYBELL: No shit.

GYNA: Let me just get the swab for residue check…
You're going to feel a slight scraping… *(She whistles a few bars of "She'll be coming round the mountain when she comes"…)*

(GYNA hands a few swabs to the NURSE who bags and tags them.)

GYNA: And now I'm going to do a visual check— *(She adjusts the exam light pointed at MAYBELL's vagina.)* What the…

(The NURSE perks up.)

NURSE: What?

MAYBELL: What?

NURSE: Drugs?

GYNA: No.

MAYBELL: Will you stop it with the "drugs" paranoia?

NURSE: Then what are you gaping at?

GYNA: I don't know…

(The door swings open. MAYBELL's lawyer, MAXINE SHARP, is there with DETECTIVE 1.)

DETECTIVE 1: Dr Scott? The perp's lawyer is here—

MAYBELL: It's about fucking time!

GYNA: Huh?

DETECTIVE 1: Did you find anything?

MAYBELL: And I'm not a perp!

NURSE: Dr Scott?

MAXINE SHARP: That means you need to cease and desist with your pelvic examination immediately.

DETECTIVE 1: Dr Scott?

GYNA: She's clean.

MAYBELL: I told you I would be. I told you. I told all of you—

DETECTIVE 1: We still need to test the swab.

MAXINE SHARP: Can you please un-cuff my client?

(DETECTIVE 1 *complies.*)

(GYNA *looks stymied…*)

GYNA: We'll run the swab for drugs and STDs, can't be too safe these days.

MAYBELL: Where's Chow? Is she okay?

(DETECTIVE 1 *snorts at mention of* CHOW's *name.*)

DETECTIVE 1: You mean Amber?

MAXINE SHARP: She's fine. Let's get you out of here and you can both fill me in—

GYNA: Here's the brochures I mentioned.

MAYBELL: Fuck you. (*But she takes the brochures on her way out the door anyway.*)

(DETECTIVE 1 *takes the bagged swab from the* NURSE.)

DETECTIVE 1: Thanks for coming in. I hope we didn't mess with your plans or anything, it being a Saturday night and all—

NURSE: You think she's a dealer or something?

DETECTIVE 1: Her? No way. More likely her friend's the dealer. We just needed a reason to get some DNA. We think maybe she has something to do with this missing guy she hooked up with last night. According to his roommate, the dude doesn't like to use condoms—

(GYNA *is still staring into space.*)

DETECTIVE 1: Hey, you okay?

(*Finally snapping to:*)

GYNA: Yeah, I'm...weird. I mean, I'm fine. She was weird.

NURSE: Aren't they all?

DETECTIVE 1: Yeah. Hey, like I was saying, since it's Saturday night and all, do you maybe wanna grab a drink?

GYNA: Are you hitting on me?

DETECTIVE 1: Yes.

GYNA: I've got a date.

DETECTIVE 1: You don't have to act offended—

GYNA: I'm not offended. I'm late. For a date. You got everything here, Sue?

(The NURSE *sighs.)*

NURSE: Yes.

*(*GYNA *grabs her purse off the table, notices the speculum is missing.)*

GYNA: Do you see the... *(She looks down around/on the ground/etc.)* Son of a bitch!

*(*DETECTIVE 1 *is admiring* GYNA's *rear...)*

NURSE: Do I see what?

*(*GYNA *glares at* DETECTIVE 1, *grabs her purse and snaps back:)*

GYNA: Never mind. *(She leaves.)*

Full House

(Six men float in space whilst playing poker. They are peculiarly dressed... It seems they too have arrived here naked or nearly so. A lucky one or two have fashioned crotch-cover for themselves out of a shredded shirt or pair of underwear that made the journey with them, but most of

them are just naked. Or, they would be naked, if it weren't for their clever use of tampons as impromptu loin cloths.)

(A few of the guys have gotten more creative with the tampons—using them as necklaces and maybe a head-dress or two. One of these head-dressed gentleman has a prominently placed dildo smack dab in the middle of his creation. His name is LEON, *and he is dealing the cards.)*

(Because they don't have a table, KUMAIL, *an unfortunately lanky dude with a wide back, floats on his hands and knees—prepared to host The River [of cards] —while* LEON *deals.)*

*(*JARED *lounges on an alligator float [the kind you'd use in a pool].)*

LEON: Alright, who's in?

(The dudes reply with a variety of "Me", "I am", "Yo", and "Why not?" before tossing a variety of vibrators into the "pot" on KUMAIL's *back...or next to* KUMAIL. *Because, maybe there's not enough room for both a pile of vibrators and a series of cards on his back...)*

LEON: Dueces are wild—

(They all groan.)

JARED: No wild cards.

LEON: It makes the game more exciting.

KUMAIL: We talked about this dude—wild cards are for babies.

LEON: Since when do tables talk?

ELI: Just let him deal the way he wants.

LEON: Thank you, Eli.

JARED: Eli's got a two.

ELI: I do not.

NICOLÁS: Then why are you defending him?

ELI: Because he's just going to bitch about it until we all give in, so why not just give in now so we can play the damn game?

NICOLÁS: If we're going to let the dealer set whatever rules they want, then why did we just spend, like, three hours setting up new rules?

ELI: It wasn't that long—

JARED: You don't know how long it was.

BEN: That's what she said.

(All them men react—a few of them un-clip tampons from their loincloths to hand to BEN.)

LEON: Nice.

BEN: Thank you.

LEON: I think the rules thing makes everyone a little grumpy.

KUMAIL: Is this going to be a long debate?

JARED: You're what's making everyone grumpy.

LEON: No I'm not.

BEN: Cool it, you two. Leon, just deal the rest of the damn cards.

(JIM floats in and stops in his tracks.)

JIM: Blanket, Blanket, Blank—

BEN: Oh Christ, here's another one.

KUMAIL: That's what she said.

BEN: *(To KUMAIL)* Dude, no. This is why you're the table.

NICOLÁS: 'Sup, dude?

JIM: What the hell is this?

ELI: Didn't we just break Jared in?

JARED: Nicolás?

NICOLÁS: Not it.

JARED: Ben?

BEN: Fuuuck, no.

JARED: Kumail—

KUMAIL: I'm the table!

JIM: Can someone tell me where I am?

LEON: It's Eli.

ELI: How you figure?

LEON: I'm the one who did—I mean, *educated*—Jared.

BEN: Good catch.

LEON: Thank you.

JIM: Hello?

JARED: Yeah, yeah, don't get your scrote in a knot.

KUMAIL: Eli?

ELI: Let's just finish the round first.

JARED: I told you he's got a two!

ELI: I do not.

JARED: Then why are you so keen on playing?

ELI: Because.

JARED: He's got a two!

LEON: Let's just pause for a moment—

BEN: You can't pause the game. Nicolás will look at everyone's cards—

KUMAIL: If we're pausing, can I get up?

NICOLÁS: Fuck you, I will not!

KUMAIL: I'd rather not show off my asshole any longer than necessary—

JARED: That's what she said! *(He laughs uproariously.)*

(KUMAIL begrudgingly hands him a tampon.)

KUMAIL: Goddamnit.

JIM: What the fuck are you guys wearing?

(They stop and look JIM over.)

BEN: Dude looks cold.

ELI: Fine! *(He stands up.)*

(NICOLÁS sneaks a peak at ELI's cards the first chance he gets: He does, in fact, have a two.)

ELI: Hello Stranger. Welcome to space-hell-purgatory-or-heaven

BEN: It's not heaven.

LEON: Shhh.

ELI: *(Not missing a beat)* I'm Eli, this is Leon, Ben, Nicolás, Kumail, and Jared.

(JARED holds up two fingers, then makes the "I'm watching you" gesture with them. ELI rolls his eyes.)

ELI: We don't know why we're here, or even where here is, but we do know this: All of us slept with the same women before waking up here, naked, alone, and scared—

NICOLÁS: I wasn't scared.

BEN: Dude—

JARED: Everyone's different.

ELI: Over time we've managed to band together and come up with some ground rules for this new society. First rule is: No man need be naked unless he wants to.

LEON: Hell's to the fuckin' yeah!

(With that, all the guys throw a few of their tampons onto KUMAIL's back. ELI steps in to tie them together, but NICOLÁS stops him.)

ELI: What?

NICOLÁS: Ben should do it—

ELI: Why?

JARED: He's better.

ELI: That's not true—

LEON: You try to make a dick-cover, we'll all be staring at the newbie's snake for days.

ELI: Fuck you—

KUMAIL: He's right.

BEN: So why do I gotta do it?

NICOLÁS: You got a skill, man. Just use it.

(BEN grumbles, but takes the tampons and begins fashioning a loin cloth for JIM.)

JARED: What's your name, bro?

JIM: Jim.

LEON: What day is it?

JIM: What?

LEON: The date. What was it when you banged her?

JIM: I'm sorry, I'm so fucking confused right now—

KUMAIL: That's because Eli sucks at this.

ELI: You think you can do better, than do better. *(He sits down.)*

(KUMAIL gives up his table duty, the cards scatter, everyone groans.)

KUMAIL: Jim, I know your mind is like, exploding right now. You were having a good time, feeling good, getting your rocks off with Maybell, when—

NICOLÁS: —That bitch—

LEON: Goddess.

BEN: We're not in heaven, dumbass.

LEON: You don't know where we are.

BEN: Exactly!

ELI: That doesn't even make sense—

KUMAIL: Dudes, not with the N-E-W-B-I-E!

JIM: I can spell.

KUMAIL: *(Talking over everyone)* —When next thing you know, BAM! You're floating in space, naked and confused, holding your balls like a newborn man-babe.

(JIM looks down at his hands clutching his balls.)

JIM: Yeah...

KUMAIL: We're all here because the exact same thing happened to us. Some of us less naked than others—

ELI: I still had my shirt, but I sacrificed it to the greater good.

LEON: I had my pants around my ankles.

BEN: And thank god for that! Brosef here had playing cards and Wrigley in his pocket!

(All the guys nod in appreciation and respect.)

JIM: So this is, I mean, I'm not having a bad trip or whatever-the-fuck—this is real?

ELI: As real as it smells.

BEN: Well, there's the time freeze thing—

KUMAIL: Yeah, yeah, I'm getting to that.

ELI: We still smell.

KUMAIL: As far as we can tell, whatever—or wherever—this is, it's frozen in time. No one has starved to death or died from dehydration, and Ben— who's been here the longest—still looks like the skinny nineteen year-old he was eight years ago.

JIM: Eight years?

LEON: Yeah.

JIM: You've been here for *eight years*?

LEON: Yep.

KUMAIL: You're welcome to look around—

JIM: EIGHT FUCKING YEARS?

BEN: Show him the zucchini.

(JARED *rummages around in his alligator float, pulls out a zucchini with reverence.*)

BEN: When I arrived, all that was here were a bunch of tampons, that alligator thing, and this bright green zucchini.

KUMAIL: Green as it ever was.

(*All the dudes repeat "Green as it ever was" with various degrees of awe.*)

(JARED *gapes, SO not understanding…*)

KUMAIL: You'll probably want to go on a little walk-about, test your senses, see the vast expanse of nothing for yourself. We don't recommend you go alone just because it tends to help fend off the inevitable mind-melt if you have a "guide", so-to-speak.

(*All the dudes shout "Not it" before* KUMAIL *can.*)

KUMAIL: Which I guess will be me. If you need to look around.

(BEN *tosses* JIM *the tampon skirt.* JIM *looks at it blankly.*)

KUMAIL: When in Rome, dude.

(*Black*)

Gyna the Gyno Has a Date

(GYNA *sits down, she is late.*)

GYNA: Sorry, sorry—are you Bud? You look exactly like your profile pic—brawny and blurry, hahaha. Sorry, I'm late. I am usually exactly on time, but I had to swing by county to do a "swab and check", otherwise I would have been here a few minutes early, probably. Freshen up my lipstick, you know, get a drink…and I would have picked one of those tables by the window. See the waitresses going in and out of that door over there? It's the kitchen, so they absolutely can't ignore you if you're sitting in one of the window tables. But this is fine. I mean, you'll see—they're just not as attentive over here. What are you drinking by the way? Vodka? I like vodka. (*She waves, shouts.*) I'll have the same as him. (*Apparently not understood*) What he's having. Right here! (*Looks back to* BUD) Is that our waitress? Whatever, it doesn't matter—she'll pass the message along. Anyway, sorry, my mind is going a mile-a-minute. It's just this damn, junkie vagina—Well, I don't know… She says she's not a junkie. She didn't look like a junkie. But do all junkies look "junkie"? I'm betting not. Otherwise we'd all know who's on the junk. Jesus, this job is jading me. Whatever, I've got a case of the heebie jeebies and I can't shake the feeling that I just like, *witnessed* something. And not in the illegal, "Hey, guards, she's got coke up the wazoo in here!" kind of way, but like, in a "That was one straaaaange vagina!" kind of way, you know? I've never felt like this after doing an exam—like I'm missing something important, but also kind of like I don't want to know what it is I'm missing. But not in a "What if she has HPV?" kind of way. It's just more like a, "Maybe that vagina is beyond my pay-grade!" kind of feeling. Except I get paid pretty well, and I'm the only one doing vaginal checks for the police right now, so there isn't anyone above my pay grade when it comes to this sort of thing, soooo… Are you eating? Did you order food? They have this killer bang-bang shrimp appetizer, or the gravy martini? It's mashed potatoes and gravy in a martini glass. I think I need food. Comfort food… Something to shove in my mouth so I'll at least stop talking— *(She looks at the menu, but can think only of the mystery vagina…)* I can't— The menu is right in front of my face and all I can see is this chick's freaky vagina! It made me feel like I was at the edge of a vast precipice. Have you ever had that feeling? You're right next to this wide, open, cavernous…hole, and you're just like, kind of hoping that you're not going to get sucked into it? Like, "Someone else is going to handle this, right?" Right?

(Her date can't relate: he absolutely wants to get sucked into something…)

GYNA: Oh my god, what am I talking about. It's just another vagina attached to another potential-junkie/ slash/maybe-murdress, and I'm completely over-thinking things and talking too much, and thank GOD I haven't told you her name or else you'd be like, implicated or something, right? As a witness? A witness to this weird vagina you've never even met, and you'd maybe have to go to court and it would be awkward because we have this personal thing going on… Is this going to be a thing, you think? Me and you? You're not that blurry, haha. God, I need that drink. *(She looks for the fucking waitress…)* It's too early to talk about us as a "thing", isn't it? I mean, "Shut up, Gyna!" How will we get to know one another when I've got just this landslide of, multi-syllabic… It's diarrhea, right? I've got diarrhea of the— *Verbal* diarrhea? Just pouring out of my mouth? Syllable after syllable after ellipses after syllable, just running down my chin, across the table, and into your poor,

defenseless ears... And I feel feverish! I mean, I have
all these hairs on the back of my neck sticking out
right here, like follicular barbed wire... You're silently
screaming inside, aren't you? Like, "Oh My GOD, She
didn't sound this crazy online!" Aagh. It's just that I
can edit myself online, you know? Right now, what
you're getting is pure unadulterated me. Speaking
of, where is that waitress with my GD unadulterated
drink? I'm sorry, may I? *(She takes a sip of his drink.)*
Gin? You're drinking gin? Jesus, is it 1922 in here? Did
I ask for one of these? Fuck. *(She looks for their waitress,
but apparently doesn't see her.... She takes another swig
of* BUD's *awful gin anyway.)* Maybe I'm just feeling
twitchy because it wasn't until after I snapped out of
my fog that I realized the bitch stole my speculum! I
mean, who does that? What is she going to do with a
speculum? She didn't look like the back-alley type to
me. Ever since you-know-who took the funding reigns,
it's been coat hangers and dirty knives up the vajay-jay
like you wouldn't believe! But this woman? No way.
She looks like she'd faint at the first sign of blood. *(She
takes another drink from his glass, shivers.)* God, that's
disgusting.

Listen: I don't know if there's a future here, between
us, or not, and I know it's going to sound super weird,
but I just have to fucking say it. And after I do, if you
still want to sit here with me and have drinks—not that
drink, but something actually delicious—and maybe
make out a little, I'm down. I will shut the fuck up
and tonsil hockey you like a horny tween on holiday!
(She takes a breath...) I think I saw another universe
inside that woman's vagina. And not in a "maybe I'm a
lesbian" kind of way or a "maybe there's a publishable
article here" sort of thing, although maybe... No. No.
I literally think this woman's vagina is some kind
of weird gateway to outer space. A space vagina. A
vagina to space.

OH MY GOD, your face! Yes, okay, hahahahahaha. I'm hearing it now. Your ears, my ears—we're both like… "Wooooo! Crazy, party of one—your drink's ready!" Except it's not. Waitress?! Hahah. I mean, now that I've said it, out loud, to *you*—it sounds crazy. *(She waves at the waitresses…)* I'm telling you, those bitches don't give a shit about this side of the place—HEY! HEY! HEY! *(She closes her eyes, takes a breath…)* This date isn't going well, is it? It's my fault. I just…I swear to God, I saw stars! And maybe a galaxy or two? It was only for a moment, and then a wind kicked up *inside* the exam room, so I blinked—and the next thing I know her lawyer is kicking down the door to bail her out and I'm siting there like "What the fuck just happened? And where the hell is my speculum?"

I think, maybe I just need to talk about this with like, someone sciency. You're not in astrophysics or anything, are you? No, I mean, I read your profile-You're a what, a numbers analyst or something mathematical. That's not what I need right now. I need a— *(She stands up tall and shouts.)* Is anyone in here a scientist? Hello? I need a scientist. Preferably someone working in space, who knows about wormholes or black-holes or whatever the fuck type space-holes there are… Anybody? Anybody? Bueler? *(She sits back down.)* I need a drink and a goddamned scientist, in that order! *(She downs the rest of her date's beverage, grimaces…)* Okay, I'm just going to go—I'm not, I mean, unless you're into this?

(He's not.)

GYNA: Yeah, I didn't think so. Fuck. I'm always— This is my fault. You're…good looking. You let me drink from the same glass as you. You don't have herpes, or anything, do you? Good. I'll just… *(She pulls a $20 out of her purse and puts it on the table.)* You really do have to sit near the windows here if you want to get service.

Remember that. This table you picked? Might as well be in the fucking Ukraine. Alright, so...we're good, right? *(She shivers.)* Jesus, Gin. What the fuck?

Scotch Tape

(GYNA knocks on her ex's door. She holds a bottle of Scotch.)

(PETE opens the door, sees who it is, closes it.)

(She knocks again.)

PETE: *(OS)* No.

GYNA: I need you.

PETE: *(OS)* We're not doing that anymore, Gyna.

GYNA: No, not your penis. I need your brain.

PETE: *(OS)* Go away.

GYNA: I NEED YOUR BRAIN!

(PETE opens the door...)

GYNA: I think I saw space inside a pothead's vagina.

(PETE stares...)

GYNA: I also have scotch.

(PETE lets GYNA in.)

A Little Sugar in Your Coffee

(MAYBELL and CHOW sit inside a coffee shop. A few other customers drink coffee and sneak peeks at the women: MAYBELL has binoculars and is watching a building across the street.)

CHOW: *(Sing-songy)* People are staring.

MAYBELL: So?

CHOW: So you're on the chain for possibly murdering a dude that lives across the street. Don't you think you ought to like, *not* look like a crazy stalker too?

MAYBELL: What if he walks into the building while we're sitting here?

CHOW: Then his roommate will tell the police he's alive and we'll get a big fat apology from the Mayor.

MAYBELL: Not if he's in on it!

CHOW: What?

MAYBELL: His roommate!

CHOW: Are you still high?

MAYBELL: This could be their thing—

CHOW: You need sleep.

MAYBELL: They find unsuspecting women and ruin their lives with fake police reports and shit—

CHOW: No.

MAYBELL: You don't know!

CHOW: Drink your coffee.

(MAYBELL *takes a sip.*)

MAYBELL: It's just so fucked up.

CHOW: I know.

MAYBELL: I didn't kill him!

CHOW: I know!

MAYBELL: What are we going to do?

CHOW: Drink our coffee, calm the fuck down, and figure out how we're going to pay that lawyer—

MAYBELL: I bet he hooked up with someone else—

CHOW: Possible.

MAYBELL: And is just having repeat sex with her, again, and again—

CHOW: Two days later?

MAYBELL: While we sit here with the police up our ass—

CHOW: Up your vagina.

MAYBELL: Up my dumb fucking vagina! *(A beat as she stares, then panics…)* Oh shit!

CHOW: What?

MAYBELL: Jim's roommate.

CHOW: So?

MAYBELL: He sees me!

CHOW: Oh shit.

MAYBELL: He's coming this way…

CHOW: Let's book!

MAYBELL: He's opening the door!

CHOW: Oh my God.

MAYBELL: He's walking towards us!

CHOW: Put those stupid things down—

(CHOW wrestles the binoculars away from MAYBELL's face.)

(VINCENT makes straight for MAYBELL…)

VINCENT: What the hell are you doing here?

CHOW: Minding our own beeswax, obviously.

MAYBELL: We're looking for Jim.

VINCENT: *You're* what happened to Jim!

CHOW: Hi, we haven't met—

VINCENT: I can call the police you know.

MAYBELL: I'm not doing anything illegal.

CHOW: I'm Chow—

VINCENT: Maybe not. But maybe so.

CHOW: Best friend and sidekick to the suspect.

MAYBELL: I'm trying to find him.

CHOW: We've been walking all morning, thought we'd stop in for coffee and what do you know, it's right here across from your apartment—

VINCENT: You're spying on me?

CHOW: No—

MAYBELL: We're spying on your building.

VINCENT: What did you do with him? Huh? What did you do with Jim?

MAYBELL: Sex. I just did sex. Shitty, shitty sex, sex—

(CHOW *can't help but laugh.* VINCENT *frowns.*)

MAYBELL: And then he booked it and he didn't even say goodbye—

CHOW: He left his pants.

VINCENT: What?

CHOW: He. Left. His. Pants.

VINCENT: That doesn't make sense.

MAYBELL: That's what *I'm* saying!

CHOW: It happens more often than you'd think.

(VINCENT *finally looks at* CHOW, *skeptically.*)

VINCENT: You the other one they arrested?

CHOW: I was taken in for questioning alongside my bestie here, but no one was arrested—

MAYBELL: There's no body.

CHOW: Jesus, May—

MAYBELL: Because nothing happened to him! At least not on my watch. He slept with me and then ditched me —

CHOW: And his pants.

VINCENT: *Something* happened to him—

CHOW: Yeah, well, when you walk around downtown without pants on…

(A "ding" as GHAZAL, *a woman wearing a headscarf enters, walks to the counter.)*

GHAZAL: I'd like a chai latte please.

MAYBELL: Listen, we just thought—

CHOW: You.

MAYBELL: Yeah, thanks, I thought—

BARISTA: No.

GHAZAL: Excuse me?

MAYBELL: That if we retraced his steps, maybe we would find some sign of him—

BARISTA: I don't serve members of the Muslim Brotherhood.

CHOW: The fuck did I just hear?

GHAZAL: I'm not—

VINCENT: Shh.

MAYBELL: What?

BARISTA: You come to our country, pushing your Sharia law crazy talk. You should be ashamed of yourself, covering up your hair like it's something to be ashamed of. I don't have to serve you. We're a private establishment. I do not condone your belief system.

CHOW: Nice neighborhood you got here—

*(*VINCENT *steps towards the* BARISTA.)*

VINCENT: Shut up.

CHOW: Oh shit.

BARISTA: Excuse me?

VINCENT: You sound like a total dick. And you don't know what your talking about. So I said shut up.

BARISTA: You can't talk to me like that!

VINCENT: Then you can't talk to her like that.

BARISTA: I can talk to her how I want to talk her, I work here.

VINCENT: Well I eat here, so I can talk to you however *I* want to, and I say shut the fuck up.

(Nobody is listening:)

GHAZAL: It's fine, I'll go somewhere else—

BARISTA: I—

VINCENT: Listen, ass-wipe, I served in the United States Army, and I didn't spend months in the motherfucking hot-ass dessert with sweat running down my crack on a daily fucking basis, with, just, swamp-ass for *months*, while extremist fuckwads tried to kill me—all in the name of defending democracy—just so it could be perverted by ignorant jack-holes like yourself.

BARISTA: Thank you for your service.

VINCENT: Shut up. You want to live somewhere where you get persecuted for your religion so you can walk around with a *real* cross on your back? Move. But as far as this country's concerned, we're all free to believe as we please, so wipe that judgmental smirk off your face and make this woman a goddamned hot beverage!

BARISTA: You're using a lot of, rough, language that is, really, unfair considering I'm working right now and not able to respond with the same, with something similar (not that I talk like that anyway—)

VINCENT: You know what? Not worth it.

(VINCENT *turns to* GHAZAL, *hands her a wad of cash.*)

VINCENT: Here. Go to Starbucks down the street—

GHAZAL: You don't have to—

BARISTA: Hey, hey—

VINCENT: Order whatever you want and then some. Shit, why don't you buy everyone in here a drink.

BARISTA: You're over-reacting—

VINCENT: Hey, everyone who isn't a racist, bigoted, bag of dicks—meet—what's your name?

GHAZAL: Ghazal.

VINCENT: Meet Ghazal at Starbucks for free drinks, right now. My treat.

BARISTA: Wait, wait, that's not fair—

VINCENT: You didn't want her business, remember?

BARISTA: But—

VINCENT: Seriously, this is happening. Free. Mother-fucking. Drinks. At Starbucks. Go.

(*People applaud, cheer, get up and move out.*)

CHOW: Oh my God, that was the hottest thing I've ever seen.

(*Someone throws their cup at the* BARISTA…)

VINCENT: Not you. That was uncalled for. We're not animals for god's sake.

(*The cup-thrower pauses, ashamed.*)

(MAYBELL *and* CHOW *start to follow the crowd out, but* VINCENT *stops them.*)

VINCENT: And not you.

MAYBELL: I didn't murder Jim.

CHOW: I just ovulated so hard!

MAYBELL: I swear to god. I couldn't murder anyone.

CHOW: I'm serious. I'm in heat over here!

MAYBELL: I faint at the first sight of blood.

CHOW: She can't even look at her own period blood without gagging.

MAYBELL: Jesus, Chow!

CHOW: What? It's true.

VINCENT: That's fucked up.

CHOW: Every month, when Aunt Flo shows up, squeamy here's riding the rag train while holding back chunks—

MAYBELL: CHOW!

CHOW: I'm sorry. My adrenaline's up and I can't stop talking—

VINCENT: If you didn't murder him, then why hasn't he come home?

MAYBELL: I don't know. Maybe he has a girlfriend or a secret wife—

(VINCENT *snorts.*)

MAYBELL: Maybe he's in the fucking CIA and got called in on some top secret mission—

VINCENT: Impossible.

MAYBELL: I'm saying I don't know the guy! But you do. Maybe, *maybe,* if you help us, we can find out what happened to him together?

(VINCENT *looks at the women…thinks for a moment…*)

VINCENT: I'm not buying you drinks.

CHOW: *You* don't have to. Ghazal's got your cash, remember?

VINCENT: Fuck.

Space...Space...and More...Space

(JIM *and* KUMAIL *wander the vast space bubble inside—or on the other side of—*MAYBELL's *vagina.*)

JIM: This can't be real.

KUMAIL: It is.

JIM: It doesn't make sense.

KUMAIL: It doesn't.

JIM: It can't be real.

KUMAIL: It is.

JIM: How in the holy hell—

KUMAIL: You're kind of on a loop here—

JIM: It can't—

KUMAIL: It is, it is, it is, itisitisitisitisitisitisitis, IT! IS!

(JIM *stares.*)

JIM: You don't have to yell at me—

KUMAIL: I'm sorry. It's just—look, I know it's, like, mind-blowing, and contrary to everything we grow up thinking can happen. If we're dead, where are the women? Were the Mormons right? And us not being Mormon, are we like, separated from the women as punishment? Leon is an ex-Catholic—Were the Catholics right? Is this Purgatory? What about karma and all that shit? Are we in a recycle bank somewhere? And what about the fact that all of us slept with the same woman? If we were really dead, wouldn't there be other non-Mormons or ex-Catholics or Hindus or Sikhs or some fucking women in with us? And why, in the name of all that's holy, are there so many goddamn dildos here? I mean, it's a giant fucking mind-melt.

JIM: So how do you stay sane?

KUMAIL: A lot of us have found religion.

JIM: Excuse me?

KUMAIL: Well, I know it doesn't make sense...and existentialism definitely has the majority. I mean... *(He gestures around him, like, "Duh"...)* But some of us feel like maybe we're doing sexual penance. I was a pretty, I don't like to talk about it really, but I've done some things I'm not proud of. Treated women like, well, you know- Being stuck in here for so long, gives you time to sort through some of that. So maybe the "What" isn't as important as the "Why" and that has given some of us a sense of purpose, you know?

JIM: No. I don't know. I don't know what you're talking about or why you think any of the shit you're saying is helpful at all. You keep calling this "The Other Place" and talking about "Gods" and "Meaning" and shit— How is any of this possible? I had a life, and now I have a...a what? A skirt made out of tampons and a bunch of freak dudes talking at me about regretting their subconscious misogynism?! Fuck this shit! And fuck you! And FUCK THIS PLACE!

(Suddenly a flying speculum zooms in and hits JIM square in the head.)

(He goes down like a ton of bricks.)

KUMAIL: Aww, man. I hate it when that happens.

Maybell Meets a Scientist

(MAYBELL's apartment. It's late and she is frantically Googling missing persons, JIM's name, and "What to do if you're accused of murder". It's late, and she's a mess.)

(A knock at the door...)

(MAYBELL *considers ignoring it…*)

(*Knock, knock, knock…*)

(MAYBELL *considers that it could be* JIM. *She squares her shoulders and gets up…*)

(*But what if it's the police again?*)

(*She pauses, frightened…*)

(*Knock, knock, KNOCK, KNOCK.*)

(*Goddamnit,* MAYBELL—*put on your big girl panties and open the freaking*—)

(*She opens the door.*)

MAYBELL: Are you freaking kidding me?

(*It's not* JIM.)

(*It's* GYNA *the Gyno and her Space Boyfriend,* PETE.)

GYNA: Good, she remembers me.

MAYBELL: Why wouldn't I remember you? You jammed your hand up my vag like I was a grab bag at the world's worst party.

GYNA: I was just doing my job—

MAYBELL: How are you even here? How do you know where I live?

PETE: You didn't tell her we were coming?

GYNA: She would have bolted—

PETE: This is highly inappropriate.

MAYBELL: Agreed!

GYNA: I may have inappropriately lifted your address from your police file, but it's because I want to help you—

MAYBELL: Sure. Right. I totally believe you—

GYNA: I don't think you killed your boyfriend.

MAYBELL: He wasn't my—wait, you don't?

PETE: Don't get all ewey gooey. She thinks your vagina is a black-hole.

MAYBELL: What?

GYNA: Can we come in?

(MAYBELL *thinks about it…*)

(*Black*)

On the Table Again…

(MAYBELL *lies back while* GYNA *and* PETE *ready themselves for an inspection.*)

MAYBELL: This is the stupidest thing I've ever done.

GYNA: I could be saying that about what *I'm* about to do—

PETE: Mhmm.

GYNA: Shut up.

PETE: I am only here for the scotch. And because you promised never to ever again knock on my door if I did this for you.

MAYBELL: Well I'm only here because it will help my lawyer argue harassment by the city—

GYNA: You guys! Shut up. I realize this is highly unorthodox and borderline crazy, but you're already here so can you just, like, go with it?

PETE: I'm going with it. I'm ready. Show me the big hole.

MAYBELL: Hey!

PETE: No, I meant— She called it a space-hole earlier… You know what, forget it.

GYNA: Have you got the camera?

PETE: Yeah, it's attached to this little cable here. Maybell, you won't feel a thing, it's like, smaller than the smallest dick imaginable—

GYNA: Jesus, really Pete?

PETE: It's super tiny.

MAYBELL: That's what she said! Hey!

GYNA: I have said that, actually. But even a teeny-tiny penis can be felt, dumbass.

PETE: It can?

GYNA: The vaginal wall is super sensitive. It's THE MOST sensitive area on the female body. How are you surprised by this?

PETE: I'm not the expert on female anatomy!

GYNA: No shit. *(Eyeroll. She addresses* MAYBELL.*)* So, listen, I'm going to do everything I did the other day— standard speculum insertion (I want it back this time though, haha)—

MAYBELL: What?

GYNA: —and a visual check. But instead of inserting my fingers—

PETE: Hot.

GYNA: —or a swab, I'll insert the camera. Meanwhile, Pete here will be watching the monitor.

PETE: You can watch it too. It's right here.

GYNA: Any questions?

MAYBELL: Exactly how much Xanax are you NOT taking right now?

GYNA: Direct your snark inwards, Maybell. You're the one who came along for the ride. Pete?

PETE: Yeah, yeah.

GYNA: Okay, here we go…

(MAYBELL *looks upwards, rolls her eyes, sighs, and eventually looks at the monitor.*)

GYNA: Okay, pushing past the vaginal opening and scooting towards the cervix—

MAYBELL: Wow.

GYNA: You aint' seen nothing yet.

PETE: Don't have to tell me that.

MAYBELL: Hey!

PETE: I meant, space. I don't see space. Jesus.

GYNA: Shhh.

(*The video shows them approaching the cervix.*)

(*It looks like a regular, every day cervix.*)

(GYNA *squints.*)

GYNA: Hmmm…

PETE: (*Dryly*) Oh Copernicus, Copernicus, it's the breakthrough of the century at last.

GYNA: Maybe…

(GYNA *pushes the camera into* MAYBELL'*s cervix…*)

MAYBELL: What are you doing?

GYNA: Last time, it wasn't until after I'd swabbed you that things seemed…weird.

MAYBELL: Well cool it with the knocking around in there, okay?

PETE: You can actually feel that?

GYNA: OhMyGod, of course she can! (*Eyeroll*)

(*The camera bumps up against the cervix a few times.*)

(*Everyone waits a beat…*)

(*Nothing happens*)

PETE: You forgot to say "Open Sesame"—

GYNA: Hmm, maybe if I just…

(GYNA *bumps the camera against the cervix again…a little harder this time.*)

MAYBELL: I'm not a fucking piñata!

GYNA: Sorry—

(*Suddenly we see the cervix contract, open just a crack, and the camera gets sucked through, pulling the cable with it…*)

PETE: Holy shit—

MAYBELL: What?

(*A slight wind picks up and the screen flashes a photo of space, then black as the cable unplugs and disappears up into* MAYBELL'*s vagina.*)

GYNA: Did you see that?! DID YOU SEE THAT?!

MAYBELL: What the hell just happened?

PETE: Impossible!

GYNA: I think you mean "Improbable", Mr Science. I WAS RIGHT!

PETE: I didn't see—I mean, it could just be a, a…

GYNA: What could it "just" be, Pete?

MAYBELL: Hello? Woman on the table would like to be part of the conversation—

PETE: This doesn't make any mathematical sense. There's no way a woman could be carrying a, a, a…

GYNA: Except that she is.

PETE: Do you have any idea what this means?

GYNA: That I was right!

MAYBELL: Hey, nerds, stop geeking out and tell me what the fuck just happened!

GYNA: Sorry Maybell, you just don't know the incredible feeling of vindication I'm riding right now.

It's like I'm high. Is this what being high feels like?
Like, I'm on top of the world and my endorphins are
just *surging*—

(MAYBELL *glares.*)

GYNA: Sorry. Pete? What does this mean?

(PETE *is rewinding and re-watching the footage…*)

PETE: It means everything we know about Einstein-
Rosen bridges is about to be called into question. It
means everyone, and I mean EVERYONE, is going to
want in on this. Astroscience, quantum theorists, the
string theory guys—Great Carl Sagan, I'm going to get
to meet the top brass… We need radiation badges. *(He
starts texting.)*

MAYBELL: Radiation?

GYNA: I think what he's trying to say is that it's very
possible you sucked your boyfriend into space through
your vagina.

MAYBELL: For the last time, Jim wasn't my- What?

GYNA: He's missing, you just sucked a camera through
there—

MAYBELL: A tiny camera.

PETE: A scope.

GYNA: Into space. Through your vagina.

MAYBELL: Jim was a full grown man.

GYNA: Yeah— Do you think he folded up, or,
ohmyGOD, what if he was pulverized into a man-meat
shaped straw or something?

MAYBELL: WHAT THE FUCK ARE YOU TALKING
ABOUT?

PETE: We need to get her to my lab.

GYNA: Whatever happened to Jim, it's obvious that you didn't do it on purpose. I mean, Pete and I can testify to that much at least—

PETE: We don't know that.

GYNA: What?

PETE: We don't know anything about her vagina except that it appears to have some sort of quantum abnormality—

GYNA: Did we not just watch the same—

PETE: You can't discern intent from that.

GYNA: Look at her face! She has no idea what's going on—

PETE: Look at her vagina—it's eating people!

MAYBELL: Whoa, whoa, whoa!

GYNA: Finally, your intimacy issues go on full display—

PETE: *(Overlapping)* —Don't make this about me—

GYNA: —I mean, Vagina Dentata? Really Pete? Is this why I never came?

MAYBELL: Whoa, what?

PETE: I am not afraid of vaginas. Maybe that vagina, but no one else's—

MAYBELL: You guys, I'm really feeling uncomfortable here.

GYNA: Sorry Maybell. Pete and I have a pretty torrid past.

PETE: No, we don't.

MAYBELL: I'm really tired, my head hurts, you're both freaking me out about, man-straws and space...I think you two need some alone time and I need to, a moment to myself to just, like, think.

PETE: You're not going anywhere.

(PETE's phone beeps, he texts some more…)

MAYBELL: Excuse me?

GYNA: I have to agree with Pete on this one. You shouldn't just walk around out there without understanding what you've got going on under your hood—

MAYBELL: You two haul me in here, scare me with the old "Camera disappears up the vagina" trick—

GYNA: *(Overlapping)* I don't think that's an "old trick"—

MAYBELL: —and now I'm supposed to stay here while you two bicker? No way!

GYNA: No one's saying you have to stay.

PETE: I am. I am saying that.

GYNA: No one besides Pete is saying you have to stay—

MAYBELL: Fuck you, Pete.

PETE: No, no fuck me. I'm not going anywhere near your vagina, and no one else should be for that matter either.

MAYBELL: I've been walking around just fine, the world has been just fine, everything will be just fine, if I leave—

PETE: How can the world be "fine" if your boyfriend got sucked into space?

MAYBELL: IF. IF. IF. And for the last time, Jim wasn't my—

GYNA: I think the odds are pretty good he's out there, girl.

MAYBELL: Because you lost a scope up my vagina?

GYNA: Cervix.

PETE: Wormhole.

MAYBELL: Are you listening to yourselves? I'm probably going to need to go to the emergency room now to get the camera removed before it ties a noose around my ovaries— *(She furiously starts getting dressed…)*

GYNA: Do you really not know what your own female reproductive system looks like?

PETE: Do you know what entering space without the proper protection would do to a man?

MAYBELL: Both of you, please, just shut up!

PETE: There's no air in space! And it's very, very—I mean, there's no way to fully articulate how— It's just damn fucking cold! Roughly 2.7 Kelvin, which is -270.45 Celsius (-454.81 Fahrenheit if you can't do the conversion), so when you sucked him into space through your monster vagina there, if he didn't get squished into an instant meat-sack, he would have been able to feel his body freeze while he was being asphyxiated—

GYNA: That's pretty gruesome—

PETE: No shit.

MAYBELL: Whatever. You two have fun discussing your shared sci-fi delusion. I'm going to the hospital for what will surely be the most expensive well-woman visit ever, and then I'm going to file a report with the city, and you're both going to get hauled into court for this, this, perversion—

PETE: I'm afraid you're not doing anything of the sort.

MAYBELL: Excuse me?

GYNA: We can't make her stay—

MAYBELL: Exactly.

PETE: Yes we can.

(The sound of heavy footsteps outside, and then the door bursts open…)

(Imposing men in black suits stand at the door.)

GYNA: Shit, Pete, I thought you worked at the community college.

PETE: That's because you constantly underestimate me.

MAYBELL: What the fuck—

PETE: Sorry, Maybell. You just became official NASA property.

(Black)

Yours, Mine, Hers, Ours, and Theirs

(A couple days later…)

(MAYBELL and her lawyer sit in a courtroom with various government officials, a freakin' federal prosecutor, GYNA, PETE, and a judge.)

(It's kind of…ridiculous.)

(Everyone is grousing about something…probably MAYBELL's vagina.)

THE CLERK: All rise! The court is now in session. The Honorable Judge Jon Jenkins presiding. The matter of the United States v. Maybell Marks will now be heard.

JUDGE JENKINS: You may be seated. Counsel, please state your appearances.

DISTRICT ATTORNEY BUCHANAN: Good afternoon, Your Honor—

JUDGE JENKINS: Is it?

DISTRICT ATTORNEY BUCHANAN: Uh, District Attorney Miles Buchanan for the state—

JUDGE JENKINS: Great. And you are?

MAXINE SHARP: Maxine Sharp, with Sharp and Associates, for the defendant.

JUDGE JENKINS: Excellent. Now then, Ms Marks, if at any time during these proceedings there is anything that you do not understand, you may pause things in order to ask the court or your attorney to explain it to you. I'll start: Ms Sharp, it's my understanding that you and the DA took it upon yourselves to agree on a plea agreement, which would let this little lady and her man-eating vagina—

MAYBELL: "Man-eating"?

JUDGE JENKINS: —loose in one of our fine state-run penitentiaries for a few months.

GYNA: (*To* MAYBELL) It's not "eating" them.

MAYBELL: Shut up.

JUDGE JENKINS: How exactly did that happen?

DISTRICT ATTORNEY BUCHANAN: Ms Marks admitted fault for the six missing men, and the state conceded that no malicious intent was involved in their disappearance—

JUDGE JENKINS: Amazing. This woman wakes up one day to find out her vagina is a serial man-gobbler—

MAYBELL: It's a "Gobbler" now?

JUDGE JENKINS: —and you two just shrug your shoulders and sign a plea agreement.

DISTRICT ATTORNEY BUCHANAN: No one "shrugged" their shoulders—

MAXINE SHARP: With all due respect, your honor, Ms Marks' vagina isn't "eating" men. It's sending them to outer space. And none of us is shrugging our shoulders at the seriousness of her situation—a situation that is absolutely unprecedented—

JUDGE JENKINS: It's terrifying.

MAYBELL: *(Under her breath)* You're telling me!

MAXINE SHARP: It's unprecedented *and* terrifying—for Ms Marks as well. She has experienced deep emotional and psychological pain in coming to grips with the fact that her vagina houses a wormhole to space—

JUDGE JENKINS: So the state is empathetic to Ms Marks plight. Fine, fine. What I don't understand, however, is why in pluperfect hell two such empathetic attorneys as yourselves would decide that it's a good idea to let this woman into one of our fine state-run jails with a goddamn ticket to space between her legs?

MAXINE SHARP: I fail to understand how the abilities of my client's vagina is grounds to nullify a plea agreement—

JUDGE JENKINS: *I'm* nullifying it on the grounds that your client is a danger to herself and everyone around her, including the poor incarcerated bastards currently in the care of our penitentiary system—wards of this state for whom we are guardians, not flight attendants.

(A titter...)

DISTRICT ATTORNEY BUCHANAN: Are you suggesting we go to trial?

JUDGE JENKINS: No, I am not. The last thing the public needs is to know that there's a portal to space with legs walking this earth, just waiting to suck them up and spit them out onto a star somewhere. Shoot, I don't want to know that she exists, but it's too late for me to call in sick, so here we are.

(US ATTORNEY EICHMAN stands up...)

US ATTORNEY EICHMAN: Your honor, it's come to the attention of several US agencies that the anomaly currently housed inside Ms Marks' you-know-what would be wildly under-utilized were she to be incarcerated—

JUDGE JENKINS: Yeah, yeah, I know all that—

US ATTORNEY EICHMAN: US Attorney Frances Eichman, your honor.

JUDGE JENKINS: Eichman. Yes. You've been peppering my office with calls, emails, paperwork like I've never seen—

US ATTORNEY EICHMAN: I'm here on behalf of—

JUDGE JENKINS: I know who you're here with. I got all kinds of agents from all kinds of offices clogging up the hallways of this courthouse trying to get a piece of Ms Marks's you-know-what, just the same as you. I've been getting "Eminent domain!" messages on behalf of every branch of the government imaginable. I'm not concerned with all that. What I want to know, and what the public needs us to decide today, is where in the seven circles of all that is holy, we can send that thing so that no one else gets disappeared up there?

MAXINE SHARP: With all due respect, the agreement that was worked out with the DA's office was more than sufficient in addressing—

JUDGE JENKINS: Three years, probation, scrub some graffiti and promise not to have sex ever again, yadda yadda— How are you going to enforce that? You don't even having her registering as a sex offender—

MAXINE SHARP: Because she's *not* a sex offender—

JUDGE JENKINS: She sent these boys into space by having sex with them. Sounds pretty damn offensive to me. Not to mention "space" is across state lines. Why in the hell hasn't she been turned over to the Feds yet?

DISTRICT ATTORNEY BUCHANAN: Your honor, if I may? Ms Marks has been under lock and key at one of NASA's laboratories, under the supervision of a Dr Peter Sellis—

PETE: Right here, sir.

JUDGE JENKINS: Ah, yes, NASA.

US ATTORNEY EICHMAN: With all due respect, your honor, NASA has had custody of Ms Marks for several days now with little to no data to report.

PETE: That's not true.

US ATTORNEY EICHMAN: Maybe you're just not sharing it then.

PETE: I've been completely transparent with my findings thus far—

US ATTORNEY EICHMAN: I repeat, with *very little* to show for their efforts. Maybell Marks is a threat to national security! She could suck us all into that black hole of hers at any second—

JUDGE JENKINS: Jesus.

GYNA: Actually, that's not how it works—

PETE: *(To GYNA)* Shut up!

JUDGE JENKINS: Is it even safe to have her sitting here with us like this?

PETE: Yes, your honor. While it's true that small objects—a speculum, a scope camera, my assistant's pencil—*have* been sucked through Ms Marks' anomaly after minor agitations to the, uh, to her…

GYNA: Cervix, you putz.

JUDGE JENKINS: Who's that now?

GYNA: I'm her gynecologist, your honor.

MAYBELL: No she isn't.

GYNA: Yes, I am.

MAYBELL: I didn't hire her—

GYNA: The state did. Because you don't have a full-time gyno—

MAYBELL: Because my insurance sucks and all the lady clinics have been shuttered—

GYNA: Preach, girl!

MAYBELL: Fuck off.

JUDGE JENKINS: Language!

MAYBELL: *(Mutters)* Sorry.

PETE: *(Over the din)* Yes, agitations to her "cervix".

JUDGE JENKINS: NASA agitated her cervix with a pencil?

PETE: Er, no—

MAYBELL: He set it down next to my crotch while they were doing a probe thing, and schwooop, up it went.

PETE: The assistant has been reprimanded—

JUDGE JENKINS: Jesus H Christ.

MAYBELL: Word.

PETE: *(Clearing his throat)* As I was saying, the wormhole mechanism is only fully functional under, ah, the right circumstances, which we're continuing to research while we, analyze the, ah, her, anomaly.

GYNA: Vagina.

PETE: *(A hiss)* Shut it! *(He throws up some slides.)* Our initial scope wasn't powerful enough to fully transmit its trip through Ms Marks' anomaly—

GYNA: Vagina!

PETE: —but it did send back one very clear image of, well, a compression of stars, before transmission ended, which we were able to identify as the Pleiades star cluster. We are currently engineering a small, erm, insertable, satellite that we will use to confirm this location—

MAYBELL: Small, my ass!

JUDGE JENKINS: *(Over the following)* Language! I swear—where the…where is my… *(He looks for something…)*

PETE: Size doesn't seem to be an issue with your, erm, well—

GYNA: Vagina! Vagina! Just say "Vagina!"

JUDGE JENKINS: Hey! HEY! Everyone just calm down now! For crying out loud. Does anyone know where my gavel is?

CLERK: Where did you last see it, sir?

JUDGE JENKINS: If I knew that, I wouldn't be asking the entire room if they've seen it.

(Everyone looks around…)

CLERK; Do you want me to check your chambers?

JUDGE JENKINS: No, I do not. I want to get this circus over with. I'll just, I'll just say "gavel" or something, when I need to use it. Okay? We're all adults here, we don't need me to pound wood in order to get everyone to order, do we? Can you all agree to listen when I say "Gavel"? Gavel! Gavel, Gavel, Gavel. Like that? Will that work?

(Everyone nods…)

(JUDGE JENKINS looks at GYNA.)

JUDGE JENKINS: And you, stop saying "Vagina" or I'll have you found in contempt of court, you hear me?

GYNA: But I'm a gynecologist.

(JUDGE JENKINS turns to PETE…)

JUDGE JENKINS: So, NASA wants to shove a satellite up this woman's you-know-what in order to find the end of the, ah, wormhole thing?

PETE: Yes. We have already directed a number of arrays at M45, but an exact location would be more helpful.

(A general stands up.)

GENERAL AIELLO: Why do we care *where* in the Sam Hill of space her yodel gully is sending people? What we need to know is whether or not the thing is stable! What happens if she falls down, opens a black hole, and we all get sucked out into space?

PETE: That's not how—

US ATTORNEY EICHMAN: This is General Aiello, your honor—

MAXINE SHARP: With all due respect, General, that seems highly unlikely.

GENERAL AIELLO: "Seems-"

MAXINE SHARP: Ms Marks has been housing the anomaly, for at least eight years, maybe longer. Maybe her whole life—

JUDGE JENKINS: Where'd you get the eight years number?

DISTRICT ATTORNEY BUCHANAN: Ms Marks' earliest known sexual partner to have gone missing was a Benjamin Kilven, your honor.

JUDGE JENKINS: They don't *all* go missing?

DISTRICT ATTORNEY BUCHANAN: Well—

PETE: The mechanism is only fully active and powerful enough to envelop a full grown man under the right, erm, circumstances—

JUDGE JENKINS: And what are those?

PETE: Well, ah, haha, you see, ah—

GYNA: They have to make her climax.

(More tittering…)

JUDGE JENKINS: Interesting.

GYNA: I thought so.

GENERAL AIELLO: For crying out loud! Who cares if the woman is climaxing or not—she's a danger to everyone around her and should be locked away in a lead-lined room—

PETE: With all due respect, lead is only good for buffering radiation—

JUDGE JENKINS: She's radioactive?

MAXINE SHARP: No.

PETE: There's a possibility of radiation escaping when the anomaly opens—

JUDGE JENKINS: NASA has had her for, what, almost a week? And doesn't know whether or not she's radioactive?

PETE: She's been uncooperative—

JUDGE JENKINS: Why aren't you cooperating with NASA?

MAXINE SHARP: My client has rights, and that includes the right to tell NASA to shove their satellite up its own vagina instead of hers if she feels like it.

JUDGE JENKINS: I don't know about that.

US ATTORNEY EICHMAN: If it please the court, there are a number of agencies represented here today with viable plans for Ms Marks' anomaly, plans that may be more effective than NASA's "wait and see" approach.

PETE: That is a patently unfair description. We haven't had government authority to mandate cooperation—

MAXINE SHARP: Surely NASA isn't asking the Federal Government to give a pass to commit non-consensual vaginal trespass with a satellite?

PETE: You're twisting it all up—

(The rest of the courtroom can't stand it anymore and begins clamoring to be heard.)

AGENT BUNCH: Your honor, the CIA has extended an invitation to Ms Marks to join our ranks. We're very interested in her assets—

MAYBELL: My "assets"?

AGENT X: This woman's sexual organ is textbook X-Files—

GYNA: Those are real?

AGENT X: Which is why the FBI has requested Ms Marks be remanded to federal custody—

GENERAL AIELLO: Eminent Domain! Eminent Domain!

MAXINE SHARP: Ms Marks is not "property"—

AGENT X: But her space-vagina is.

AGENT BUNCH: She's a goddamned Intelligence wet dream—

GENERAL AIELLO: She's a threat to national security!

MAXINE SHARP: Ms Marks is a fucking human being with inalienable fucking rights—

JUDGE JENKINS: Language!

AGENT X: Have you seen any of those up there?

PETE: What?

AGENT X: Aliens?

JUDGE JENKINS: GAVEL, GAVEL, GAVEL!

(Everyone settles.)

JUDGE JENKINS: Absolute circus. So we've got the CIA, FBI, Army, and NASA clowns all here looking for a piece. Did I miss anyone?

US ATTORNEY EICHMAN: The Forest Service is here too, somewhere.

JUDGE JENKINS: Forest Service?

USFS CHIEF HOWE: Nope. No thanks. Withdrawn.

JUDGE JENKINS: Who said that?

USFS CHIEF HOWE: I did, your honor. US Forest Service Chief Howe. I was told we'd discovered a "New kind of bush" that was "Out of this world", and that people were "Dying" to see it—

JUDGE JENKINS: Mighty, mighty, Mickey Mouse!

USFS CHIEF HOWE: —Leading me to think there were some tourism dollars to be had—

MAYBELL: You want to send tourists up my twat?

JUDGE JENKINS: What did I just hear?

USFS CHIEF HOWE: No, I most definitely do not. It was obviously a bad joke. National Parks wants nothing to do with Ms Marks', er—

MAYBELL: Twat.

JUDGE JENKINS: God Almighty!

USFS CHIEF HOWE: —Space bush.

JUDGE JENKINS: Ms Sharp, get your client's mouth under control or I'll find her in contempt—

MAYBELL: Great. So you can throw me in jail with all the jailbirds you're so worried I'll screw? Right.

JUDGE JENKINS: Now look here, missy. I understand that you don't like us all sitting her discussing your private parts, but I am not your enemy. You can't just walk around out there in the world with that thing and expect everyone to just "deal" with it. You need to be studied, and that space between your legs regulated. So you *are* going home with one of these agencies today, no bones about it. You can either help me determine the best place for you, or you can continue to piss me off so that I pick the most uncomfortable one, got it?

(MAYBELL *narrows her eyes.*)

JUDGE JENKINS: Honestly, the way you're acting, it's like textbook millennial selfishness. There's absolutely no remorse for those poor young men you killed!

MAYBELL: Because I didn't *kill* anyone.

JUDGE JENKINS: What's that now?

DISTRICT ATTORNEY BUCHANAN: Based on evidence procured from an earlier NASA probe, it's the State's opinion that the men missing up Ms Marks' vagina are, erm, still alive.

(JUDGE JENKINS *judge looks at* PETE.)

JUDGE JENKINS: Explain.

PETE: The, ah, the guys. They're not, well, it defies all logical explanation, but really this whole situation defies all logical—

JUDGE JENKINS: The point!

PETE: They're not dead.

JUDGE JENKINS: How do you know that?

PETE: The second probe Ms Marks allowed us to insert into the, ah, wormhole... It, well, it was a little stronger than the first one I used because at first, I wasn't in a proper lab, and I didn't have access to- well, it was all personal equipment. I filled out a reimbursement form, but that's neither here nor there—

JUDGE JENKINS: Mr Sellis!

PETE: Yes, sorry. The thing is, the second probe, official NASA property, was in communication for far longer than the first. It sent back a rather startling image before cutting out.

(PETE *hits a button on his projector and brief video plays.*)

(*At first we see static, black, a few throbbing stars, and then...*KUMAIL *in all his tampon-skirt glory walks towards the camera, perplexed... He reaches for it, appears to look over his shoulder with a "Hey guys! Are you seeing this?" before grabbing the camera. As he does so, it pans right, allowing us to see a few more of the dudes looking surprised before it cuts out.*)

(*The room is silent.*)

JUDGE JENKINS: What, ah, what am I looking at here?

MAXINE SHARP: These are the missing men, your honor.

DISTRICT ATTORNEY BUCHANAN: We haven't shown this to their families yet. We're afraid it might cause distress—

JUDGE JENKINS: Are they wearing...

PETE: Feminine hygiene products, your honor. Yes. We believe they are.

JUDGE JENKINS: God almighty...

(*A beat while everyone digests the image...*)

PETE: Obviously, your honor, we all have questions—a lot of questions. And these questions need to be answered. As soon as possible. And before the public finds out about any of this. And since Ms Marks' anomaly is spacey in nature, and since these men appear to be—somehow—still alive, we feel that Ms Marks and her Vagina should be working with *us*. Let NASA get a deeper understanding of just what it is that's happening here, and then decide where her talents are best put to use.

JUDGE JENKINS: We need to bring those boys home.

US ATTORNEY EICHMAN: Sir?

JUDGE JENKINS: Those are American's out, up— *Out* there up her you-know-what. American men lost in space! I won't stand for it. Uncle Sam won't stand for it. We need to bring those boys home!

PETE: NASA agrees, sir. One hundred percent.

(JUDGE JENKINS *gives* MAYBELL *a sharp look.*)

JUDGE JENKINS: Now listen here, missy—I want you to pretend I'm pointing my gavel at you. Can you do that?

(MAYBELL *rolls her eyes.*)

JUDGE JENKINS: I'm serious! Because what I'm about to say is binding, you got me? This isn't just your life we're talking about here, it's the lives of those…five?

PETE: That we know of.

JUDGE JENKINS: Five, that we know of, brave young men inside you—

GYNA: They're in *space*.

JUDGE JENKINS: Yes, but they're in space *because* they were inside her!

GYNA: But they're not inside her now—

JUDGE JENKINS: Gavel! Gavel! Stop sassing this court, missy, or I will keep you in this courthouse forever, understand?

GYNA: Yes, sir.

(JUDGE JENKINS *looks back at* MAYBELL.)

JUDGE JENKINS: I'm remanding you to NASA for the most meticulous study that every existed. I want to know everything about your vagina- how it works, why it works, and how in the name of all that is holy, we can shut it down. But most of all, I want to know how to bring those boys back. So you're going to let NASA get all up in that vagina of yours, and you're going to be cooperative about it because if I hear even one little peep out of you, I'm going to hand you over to the General or the CIA, and let them take you to one of those black-op places that don't exist where they get so up close and personal with your vagina that they will *become* your vagina, you hear me?

MAYBELL: Jesus.

MAXINE SHARP: There were so many inappropriate things in that statement, your honor, I don't even know where to begin—

JUDGE JENKINS: You'll begin by telling your client to follow my directions. Ms Marks is NOT human rights campaign material—she has a wormhole to space inside her body. I can't think of a more fitting use of the eminent domain law than this. And if I hear even a peep out of any of you about trying to take this public, I'll ship you off to Panama so fast your heads will spin. *(He looks at* MAYBELL.*)* You are hereby ordered, by the federal government of the United States of America, to cooperate with NASA for a period not to exceed maybe the rest of your life, or until they figure out a way to shut your wormhole down. We'll reconvene in two weeks to check everyone's status. Mr Sellis, you and your NASA boys better find a way to get that satellite up Ms Marks' you-know-what ASAP, and figure out a way to bring those boys home or I'll hold the entire department in contempt of court for obstructing these boys' goddamn justice!

MAYBELL: What?

PETE: Can he do that?

DISTRICT ATTORNEY BUCHANAN: I don't think so—

MAXINE SHARP: Absolutely not—

JUDGE JENKINS: I can. I am. And I will. Get on it! Court dismissed!

END OF ACT ONE

ACT TWO

Glass Between Us

(MAYBELL *sits on one side of a plexiglass wall,* CHOW *on the other. They hold phones up to their ears in order to talk to one another.*)

CHOW: This is all so fucked up.

MAYBELL: Everyone's afraid I'll hiccup and accidentally suck someone into orbit.

CHOW: I've slept next to you—

MAYBELL: I know.

CHOW: I've been high as fuck with you—

MAYBELL: I know.

CHOW: I even helped you fish a tampon out of your space-box that one time the string came off—

MAYBELL: I know!

CHOW: And I've never even felt a hint of wormhole-suckage from your vagina!

MAYBELL: Thank God.

CHOW: I don't like talking at you from behind glass.

MAYBELL: Fuck NASA.

CHOW: Fuck the government.

MAYBELL: Fuck my vagina.

CHOW: Hey, it's not your fault your tuna canoe decided to go all sci-fi on those guys. If you ask me, some of those assholes probably deserved a little time out—

MAYBELL: But they're stuck there, Chow. Maybe forever. I'm totally dangerous.

CHOW: Shut up. You're a pussy cat. It's your pussy that's the danger. When you get out of here, you can start your own merch line— "Danger-Puss!" People will lose their minds—

MAYBELL: I'm never getting out of here.

CHOW: Sure you will! They're NASA for crying out loud. They're totally going to figure out how to remove that thing and then you'll be free.

MAYBELL: Did Pete tell you they're going to shove a four foot satellite up my slot?

CHOW: Jesus.

MAYBELL: They think that the wormhole bends the rules of gravity, space, and time all at once, and that my body will totally not rip in two when it goes through, but I'm skeptical.

CHOW: Are you, are you sure you're okay with this?

MAYBELL: I have to try, don't I? I mean, it's my fault these guys are stranded out there. If they hadn't had the terrible misfortune to have sex with me, they'd still be on planet earth, living their lives, making babies, having mind-blowing sex with their wives—

CHOW: Babies are major cock-blockers.

MAYBELL: They'd be happy, is what I'm saying. Instead of trapped in space.

CHOW: When does the satellite thing happen?

MAYBELL: Tonight. I told them I'd only do it if I got to talk to you first. I want, I want to say goodbye in case I like, die.

CHOW: Oh my GOD, you are not going to die!

MAYBELL: I might. I might. And if I do, you have got to promise me that you will burn all of my journals and erase my hard drive before my mom cleans out my apartment, okay? And take the weed. And bury my vibrators. And keep Kitty happy—

CHOW: Jesus, yes. Of course. But, Maybell—You're not fucking dying! You always bounce back, eventually. You're like, rubber.

MAYBELL: No, Chow—that's you. You're the bouncy one. I'm just a tired out hole to space.

CHOW: Shut up—

MAYBELL: You shut up! I'm serious—what is the reason for my existence? Even if I get out of here someday, I can never have sex again. I can never have kids—

CHOW: I didn't know you wanted to make babies—

MAYBELL: I didn't. But that was when it was my choice. Now that I know I can't, it's like, maybe I wanted to have the option of changing my mind later! To be able to decide to have them "some day", if I got all hormonally maternal and shit, you know? And what kind of, I mean, I was always talking about not *needing* a man, but I still kind of hoped I'd find a guy I could like, share some of my life with in a meaningful way, you know? And now that's totally out the window, unless I hunt down a fucking eunuch—

CHOW: Okay, listen to me. You are going to be fine. You can always adopt, if you decide babies are a necessary part of your future. And I'll help you with all of that! And you should also totally not knock the whole eunuch thing until you try it, okay? Maybe it sounds horrible, but not having sex might be like, your pathway to the most enlightened existence ever—

MAYBELL: Remember when we were talking about your solitude retreat?

CHOW: Yeah—

MAYBELL: That's going to be my life, Chow. The Danger-Puss line won't be funny kitsch, it'll be, like, the most depressing line of sexless dungarees imaginable. I may not need the whole marriage/babies thing, but I really enjoy making out and having sex.

(CHOW *doesn't know what else to say…*)

CHOW: I love you.

MAYBELL: I love you too. Don't forget about my journals, okay? And Kitty. And the vibrators. All of them. *All* of them, Chow.

(CHOW *lifts her hand up to the glass, pinky up…*MAYBELL *puts her pinky to the glass. Both girls kiss their thumbs in a sweet, final, glass-separated pinky swear ritual.*)

(*Beat*)

(*Beat*)

(*Dark*)

Spread 'Em!

(MAYBELL *lies on a bed with a satellite between her legs. The satellite is equipped with a large vibrator at one end. A scientist in a pressurized suit tries to activate her's vagina with the vibrator-equipped satellite…*)

(*He's tethered to the wall just in case it works…*)

(*BUT, it's all too clinical to get* MAYBELL*'s wormhole to open.*)

(*We hear a voice over the speaker… It's* PETE.)

PETE: *(VO)* What's the problem?

MAYBELL: I'm not into robots.

PETE: *(VO)* It's a satellite, not a robot—

MAYBELL: Whatever. It's not sexy.

PETE: *(VO)* We talked about this—

MAYBELL: It's also totally fucking quiet in here. I can hear every move Squeaky McGee over there is making.

NERVOUS SCIENTIST: Excuse me?

PETE: *(VO)* Would you like some music?

MAYBELL: You'd think you could have found someone less likely to shit himself—

NERVOUS SCIENTIST: I'm sorry. It's just that I'm afraid you might suck me into SPACE!

PETE: *(VO)* We could try dimming the lights?

MAYBELL: Don't you have any sexy cowboy scientists out there? Insecurity is such a huge turn-off.

NERVOUS SCIENTIST: I'm not here to turn you on—

MAYBELL: Yes, you are!

NERVOUS SCIENTIST: That's what the vibrator is for!

MAYBELL: Well, you're both shaking so much, I can't tell where one ends and the other begins. Just be careful you don't sweat through your suit and short-circuit my cooch—

PETE: *(VO)* Okay, we're all a bit nervous here. Lots of pressure. Lashing out isn't going to resolve anything. Would you like us to dim the lights, Maybell? And play some music? We can do both—

MAYBELL: Yeah. Fine. Whatever.

(They dim the lights.)

(They play some music…it's not sexy. They try a few different options before MAYBELL *is satisfied.)*

MAYBELL: No. Nope. Jesus Christ, do you guys ever fuck? No. Change it— Okay, yeah. Finally. Leave it there.

(The NERVOUS SCIENTIST *tries again…)*

(Nothing happens though.)

PETE: *(VO)* Maybell, I just don't think you're putting your all into things here—

MAYBELL: You have created the MOST UN-SEXY ENVIRONMENT EVER, and you're blaming me for not getting turned on? I can hear you mouth-breathers hanging on every flick of this idiot's clumsy-ass wrist— don't any of you watch porn? Or is this how you all like it? Sterilized and extra bright?

PETE: *(VO)* We turned down the—

MAYBELL: It's not about the fucking lights! It's about trying to fuck a satellite with a live goddamned audience watching and the fate of every dude who's ever made me come hanging in the balance. My cake box is clamping down under the pressure, okay? Drying up like a little old lady watching monkeys screw at the zoo—

(A beat…)

PETE: *(VO)* I don't know what you want us to—

*(*MAYBELL *gets up, pushing the* NERVOUS SCIENTIST *to the door and wrestling the vibrator controls from him.)*

MAYBELL: You know what? Just get out. All of you. Turn off the lights, turn off the monitors, get out and leave me alone in the dark, okay?

PETE: *(VO)* We talked about this! It's imperative that we observe the process—

MAYBELL: Well unless you want to continue to observe NOTHING HAPPENING, I suggest you adapt your expectations to the current scenario, you fucking maroon—

PETE: *(VO)* Maroon?

NERVOUS SCIENTIST: That's Bugs Bunny for moron.

MAYBELL: I need to do this alone and anything else is just you guys getting in my way.

(The NERVOUS SCIENTIST *looks up to where* PETE *and the other scientists are presumably watching and shrugs his shoulders.)*

(Finally…)

(The lab door open with a "Whoosh".)

PETE: *(VO)* Give her the instrument.

NERVOUS SCIENTIST: Thank you.

*(*NERVOUS SCIENTIST *hands over control to* MAYBELL *and scurries out of the room.)*

PETE: *(VO)* How long do you think you'll need—

MAYBELL: Haven't you ever heard the saying "A watched pot never boils", Pete? Go get yourself a cup of coffee. I'll call you all back when I'm done… providing R2-D2 here doesn't shred me into lunchmeat on his way to the stars.

(The sound of equipment shutting down…)

(The lights turn off.)

(After a moment…)

MAYBELL: Okay, Buzz, it's just you and me now, baby.

(A buzz…)

MAYBELL: To infinity and beyond…

How Do You Solve a Problem Like Space?

(The dudes sit around another man-table, this time it's JIM—*the vibrator-equipped satellite sits on his back while the gents examine it.)*

*(*NICOLÁS *jumps rope with one of the earlier probe cables.)*

NICOLÁS: It's a sex bot.

ELI: It's not a—

KUMAIL: It looks like a—

ELI: But—

JARED: Dude, it's a fucking sex-bot.

(They all look at it.)

BEN: So what does it mean?

LEON: Well, obviously we're not in purgatory.

KUMAIL: We don't know that—

LEON: You think they have sex-bots in purgatory?

KUMAIL: Well, no…

JIM: I can't believe any of you thought purgatory would be filled with tampons and dildos—

ELI: Shut up.

LEON: You haven't been here long enough to criticize our coping mechanisms.

JIM: Whatever.

*(*JARED *scrutinizes the satellite.)*

ELI: I don't think it's a sex-bot.

JARED: Dude, there's a dildo strapped to its head!

BEN: Sex-bot or no, why aren't we talking about what it's sudden appearance here *means*?

LEON: It looks like it does a lot more than just fuck.

NICOLÁS: *(With major eyeroll)* Says the scientist.

KUMAIL: It confirms that we're all here because of our sexual transgressions and we need to atone more fervently—

ELI: Or else we'll be invaded by inert sex-bots?

LEON: Whatever dude.

JIM: It means someone is looking for me.

BEN: What?

JIM: Yeah, it's like- I mean, a probe or something right? First the cameras and now this?

NICOLÁS: What makes you think anyone's looking for *you*?

JIM: I'm the last one to arrive here, right? Obviously someone figured out that Maybell has been…doing whatever it is she's been…er— *(He doesn't know what* MAYBELL *has done to them.)*

KUMAIL: Yes?

JIM: They know she's done *something* to me. And you guys too, probably.

ELI: Super helpful, dude.

*(*NICOLÁS *does some double jumps, is surprisingly good at jumping rope.)*

BEN: Can you please knock that shit off?

NICOLÁS: Why?

BEN: It's annoying the fuck out of all of us.

NICOLÁS: Really?

LEON: It's not bothering me—

BEN: You've been dicking around with that cable ever since it showed up.

NICOLÁS: It's good exercise. *(He starts adding in cross jumps.)*

BEN: Exercise for what?

NICOLÁS: For my body.

KUMAIL: No one here cares about your abs.

NICOLÁS: My glutes.

BEN: No one cares.

NICOLÁS: I care. And when we get back to Earth? All the women on Earth will care.

JARED: You really think we're going back?

NICOLÁS: One hundred percent.

JIM: Can I please get up now?

LEON: No, newbie. We're inspecting the thing.

JIM: But it's really heavy, and I don't see why it needs to be on my back instead of just like, on the ground or whatever—

BEN: Because you're super fucking annoying and need to learn humility.

JIM: Fuck you.

BEN: Fuck you.

JIM: Whatever. Just hurry up and inspect it then.

(NICOLÁS ups his jump rope game while the rest of the guys inspect the satellite.)

NICOLÁS: They'll probably put us on Ellen. Is she still on?

JIM: I don't know, dude.

NICOLÁS: I'm going to kiss her.

ELI: She's married to a woman.

NICOLÁS: I'm going to kiss her anyway.

BEN: You spend years locked away here and the first thing want to do when you get back is kiss a lesbian?

NICOLÁS: I like Ellen, okay? I used to watch her every day. When I'm having a bad day here, like right now with you pissing me off? I think about what Ellen would do or say to make the whole thing funny instead and it keeps me from strangling you until your stupid fucking eyes pop out of your big dumb skull!

LEON: Guys—

NICOLÁS: So when I see that beautiful lesbian angel? I'm going to kiss her in front of her millions of fans for helping me to NOT murder all of you! (*He does a series of double jumps…*)

KUMAIL: Let's just stop talking about Ellen, okay?

JIM: You know what, fuck this.

(JIM *stands up and the satellite falls…*)

(*But once the satellite hits the "ground", a panel pops open and a rolled up sheet of paper emerges. No one notices right away…*)

(*The guys all talk at once.*)

LEON: What are you doing?

KUMAIL: Noooo!

ELI: Wait a hot second, dick-head—

BEN: Nice going, ass-wipe. Now you broke it!

(JARED *reaches for the satellite's vibrator…*)

JARED: Dibs! (*But then he sees that the panel has popped open and picks up the paper.*)

JARED: Double dibs.

LEON: That's a really big box for such a little note.

(KUMAIL *snatches it from him.*)

NICOLÁS: What is it?

KUMAIL: It's a letter. From Maybell.

JARED: What the shit?

ELI: Anyone else feeling kind of sick to their stomachs here?

JIM: What does it say?

(The gentlemen listen as KUMAIL *reads* MAYBELL's *letter…)*

KUMAIL: "Dear Jim, Eli, Kumail, Benji—"

(The guys make "ooooh!" sounds.)

NICOLÁS: Benji? Hahahaha— You're named after a dog!

BEN: My name is Benjamin. She called me Benji—

NICOLÁS: Like the dog!

BEN: Because we were young and stupid and I thought it sounded cute when she said it.

NICOLÁS: *(He coughs)* Loser!

KUMAIL: Can I read this freaking letter already?

(Everyone shuts up.)

KUMAIL: "Dear Jim, Eli, Kumail, Benji, Leon, Nikolàs and that dude I banged at Burning Man (I'm so sorry I don't know your name. No one here knows who you are either. I hope you'll help us out with that, but more on that in a moment.)" He looks up.

KUMAIL: Shit, Jared, is that you?

JARED: Classic.

KUMAIL: "I'm really, really sorry that you're all in space. I had no idea that my vagina could do that—"

BEN: What's that now?

NICOLÁS: Her vagina did *what*?

JIM: Is this for real?

KUMAIL: I don't know man, the information is just as new to me as it is to you!

LEON: Shut up and let him read.

(KUMAIL *resumes reading…*)

KUMAIL: "I thought you had all just bailed on me after we hooked up, but now I know (even though it sounds crazy) that you were sucked out into space through a wormhole that lives inside my vagina."

LEON: See? If you just shut up, more information comes.

BEN: What the hell is a wormhole?

JIM: It's like, *Star Trek.*

ELI: Time travel and stuff. You can use it to travel through time.

JIM: Through space.

ELI: Isn't it both?

NICOLÁS: You guys are idiots.

KUMAIL: How the hell can a wormhole live in someone's vagina?

(JIM *swipes the letter.*)

JIM: "Please know that if I had had any idea, any idea at ALL that this was possible, I would have stopped having sex immediately and put my pussy on lockdown."
Ha, yeah, okay lady. Shit.
"I want you all to know that I am writing this from a lab at NASA, where a thousand super-smart people are working on how to make things right. Everyone here wants to bring you guys home."

NICOLÁS: I told you!

BEN: Shut up!

NICOLÁS: Ellen Degeneres, here I come! *(He doubles down on his jumprope.)*

JIM: "Hence, this very large satellite you're looking at right now." *(He looks at it.)* So that's what this is.

JARED: Who says "Hence"?

JIM: Who cares. It's a satellite. That means we can communicate with home, right? *(He jumps "in front" of the thing, waves his arms and shouts, his mouth incredibly close to the vibrator portion of the satellite.)*

JIM: Help! I'm trapped out here with a bunch of morons!

(KUMAIL snatches the letter back.)

KUMAIL: You're the moron.

LEON: Dude, I don't think it's on.

ELI: Are none of you still shocked by the whole, getting sent here by a vagina-wormhole, thing?

JIM: I am. Totally.

LEON: Me too.

KUMAIL: I think we all are, dude. *(He continues reading.)* Holy shit, listen to this: "I don't know how it's"—she's talking about the satellite thing- "going to get through, but if you're reading this, then it did. And hopefully it didn't rip me in two in the process, killing me and possibly collapsing the wormhole, as it made its way to you."

LEON: Holy shit.

ELI: I don't see any blood anywhere.

JIM: Yeah, me neither.

JARED: That's what she said!

BEN: Not the right time, man. At all.

NICOLÁS: Would we still be here if she died?

ELI: We don't even know where "here" is.

NICOLÁS: Inside her wormhole.

(Everyone looks at NICOLÁS.*)*

BEN: Gee, let's all pull out our wormhole PhDs so
we can give Niko here a scientific answer on the
probability of our survival if the stupid thing we didn't
even know existed until five minutes ago "dies"—

*(*NICOLÁS *sighs.)*

NICOLÁS: Whatever.

LEON: Is there anything else?

*(*KUMAIL *resumes reading.)*

KUMAIL: Just another apology and this:
"This is how sorry I am: I'm letting NASA send an
extremely large, pointy, cold, metallic structure up
my vagina, knowing that it might kill me, in order to
potentially save you guys."

JIM: Somebody hand this chick a medal.

BEN: Shut up.

KUMAIL: "I just hope that wherever you guys are, that
you're all getting along and finding a way to be happy.
I know this sucks more than anything, but at least
you're not dead, right? I mean, that has to be worth
something.
Accompanying this letter, you should find a watch, a
Sharpie, and some sheets of blank paper—"

*(*ELI *looks in the compartment, finds the marker and paper.)*

ELI: Got 'em!

KUMAIL: "NASA wants you to answer a few questions
for them, then hold the papers up at exactly 07:00 in the
same place that you found the probe and the satellite.
Assuming this satellite didn't kill me, and assuming
everything comes out my wormhole in the same place,

they'll be sending another camera through my cooch to snap pictures of your answers."

(JARED *laughs.*)

JARED: "Cooch."

(BEN *yanks one of* JARED's *tampons off and clips it to his own skirt.*)

JARED: Hey!

BEN: You're an idiot.

KUMAIL: "I guess, after that, we'll kind of keep doing this message-through-the-vagina thing until the satellite makes contact or they figure out a plan to bring you home.
Again, I am extremely sorry for how things turned out. Please know that I am doing everything in my power to make it right. Sincerely, Maybell, the Woman Whose Vagina Sends People to Space."

(*The men are quiet for a moment...except for* NICOLÁS, *who continues to jump rope.*)

(*After a moment...*)

LEON: So we're in space.

ELI: If we were just floating in space, wouldn't we be dead?

JARED: And if we're still alive, wouldn't we need to like, eat?

NICOLÁS: I haven't taken a shit in six years.

BEN: Obviously there's something...else...going on—

KUMAIL: Maybe it's a spiritual test—

NICOLÁS: Oh, man, give it a rest with that spiritual crap.

JIM: I'm with NICOLÁS on this.

EVERYONE: Shut up, newbie/Shut it!/Ugh.

LEON: No one cares who you're with, noob.

JARED: That's what she said.

(LEON *high-fives* JARED.)

LEON: Decent.

JARED: Hand 'em over.

(*The guys all hand* JARED *a tampon… Which is good, because his skirt was getting a little thin.*)

(JIM *resists…*)

JARED: Hand. It. Over.

JIM: Fuck off.

(JARED *and* JIM *continue their argument under the following:*)

ELI: So, what are NASA's questions?

(KUMAIL *reads from another piece of paper.*)

KUMAIL: Uh… "What food sources are you sustaining yourselves with? Where is your water coming from? Have you seen any other signs of life? Why does Ben look the same as he did in college? Can you draw a picture of the nearest star cluster? How are you shaving? Have any of you sustained injuries—" There are a lot more.

BEN: (*To* KUMAIL) How many more?

JARED: Dude, I nailed it.

JIM: I'm not giving you one of my tampons!

KUMAIL: Ummmmmmmm…. (*He counts.*) Forty-two?

JIM: You can already see my balls as it is!

ELI: (*To* KUMAIL) That's ridiculous.

JARED: Everyone here has already seen everyone's balls. That's not the point.

NICOLÁS: Do they say anything about how to get the stupid satellite working?

LEON: Yeah, it doesn't seem to be doing anything—

JIM: Then what is the point? Huh? What's the fucking point of the whole goddamned system?

KUMAIL: I don't see any— Oh, yeah... Push the big green button to activate.

JARED: The point is that we show respect when someone lands a particularly good "That's what she said" because *The Office* is the greatest TV show of all time, and Michael Scott, AKA, Steve Carell, is a fucking comedy genius, and I just landed a solid one, and now you owe me a goddamn fucking tampon out of respect!

LEON: *(To* JIM *and* JARED*)* What's going on with you two?

BEN: So they send us this hunk of junk satellite that we have to turn on ourselves, ask us a million questions that we don't have answers to, and then expect us to just stand around hoping to get our picture taken by the next thing they send through Maybell's Downstairs Gal?

JIM: *(To* LEON*)* He's being a whiny little prick, is what's going on.

*(*NICOLÁS *stops jumping rope.)*

NICOLÁS: The fuck did I just hear?

JARED: He's not respecting the rules.

BEN: What?

JIM: Rules that you fools made up before I got here.

NICOLÁS: Did you just call her pussy "Downstairs Gal?"

BEN: Yeah. So?

KUMAIL: Guys—

JARED: *(To* JIM*)* Exactly—*before you got here.* Meaning, you're the new guy, meaning you need to fall in line to the established way of things—

NICOLÁS: *(To* BEN*)* That's the dumbest euphemism for twat I ever heard.

JIM: *(To* JARED*)* But I don't even like *The Office!*

BEN: *(To* NICOLÁS*)* Shut up.

ELI: *(To the group)* Who doesn't like *The Office??*

NICOLÁS: *(To* BEN*)* Are you her grandma?

JARED: *(To* ELI*)* Jim.

BEN: *(To* NICOLÁS*)* Shut. Up.

ELI: *(To* JIM*)* Dude.

LEON: *(To everyone)* Guys—

NICOLÁS: You know, sometimes I almost forget you're a near-virgin—

BEN: *(Overlapping)* It's not my fault I only got to have sex twice before I got sent here!

NICOLÁS: — But then you go and say something stupid like "Downstairs Gal" and I get to laugh at you all over again!

BEN: *(To* NICOLÁS*)* Shut up!

KUMAIL: Guys!

NICOLÁS: *(To* BEN*)* Make me!

ELI: I think we're all spinning out a little bit here—

KUMAIL: I don't understand what's happening.

LEON: We all thought we were dead. Now we know we're alive, it changes everything—

JIM: I never thought I was dead.

JARED: I swear to God, if you don't hand me a fucking tampon, I'm going take your whole goddamned skirt—

KUMAIL: I think we should all try to calm down—

JIM: We just learned we're being held prisoner by a rogue vagina. I think a little bit of rage is appropriate—

BEN: What do you know about it, noob?

JIM: Don't get mad at me! *I'm* the reason NASA's looking for us!

JARED: Give it a rest, man. No one's interested in watching the "Jim" show—

JIM: You're just jealous because no one even knew you were missing!

JARED: *Someone* has noticed I'm missing!

LEON: It doesn't sound like they have—

JARED: Fuck you, Leon!

LEON: Fuck you, Jared!

JIM: That's what I've been saying!

KUMAIL: Guys, let's all just calm down—

EVERYONE: SHUT UP, KUMAIL!

(The men lunge at one another in a tussle of epic space proportions…)

(Black)

Houston, We Have a Problem

(MAYBELL sits amidst a sea of scientists, PETE stationed at the front of the herd as their leader…)

(Gyna is also in the room, looking professional.)

(They all look at a projected photo of the dudes…)

(Some have black eyes, bloody noses. The papers they're holding have been crumpled and torn in some places.)

(JIM is tied up with one of the probe cables.)

PETE: What am I looking at here?

GYNA: Looks like they had a… tussle.

SCIENTIST 1: They've gone full *Lord of the Flies* in there!

(MAYBELL *puts a hand to her stomach.*)

SCIENTIST 3: *Up* there.

SCIENTIST 2: *Out* there.

SCIENTIST 1: Right.

PETE: Weeping William Herschel!

SCIENTIST 2: Their handwriting is for shit.

(SCIENTIST 2 *hits a button and we zoom in on a series of close ups of some of the papers.*)

SCIENTIST 2: This one says "No food. No water. No idea how we're all still alive. You're the scientists."

SCIENTIST 3: My personal favorite: "ET phone home"- obviously a waste of time there.

SCIENTIST 1: We've identified the seventh gentleman at least.

(*A close up of* JARED, *whose sign reads "My name's Jared Hill, assholes".*)

MAYBELL: Jared! Yes!

PETE: The seventh gentleman.

MAYBELL: That was driving me crazy.

PETE: Too bad he didn't provide a social security number.

SCIENTIST 2: We can ask for that on the next go round.

SCIENTIST 3: Kumail has provided the most detailed answers.

(*A close up of* KUMAIL'S *paper.*)

SCIENTIST 3: "We don't know how we are still alive here. We are the only ones here. We don't know what 'here' is— We thought we were all in purgatory or awaiting our next life. None of us have aged or taken a shit… Maybe this *is* the afterlife?"

GYNA: Jesus.

PETE: What about questions 22, 23, and 27?

SCIENTIST 3: They don't seem to have even tried.

(A slide of BEN holding a sheet of paper with a bunch of dots on it…)

PETE: Is that supposed to be the star map we asked for?

SCIENTIST 1: We think so.

SCIENTIST 3: There's no differentiation in size, every dot is uniform—we can't pull anything from it.

PETE: It's shit.

SCIENTIST 2: Yes. Yes, it is.

PETE: What would Stephen Hawking do?

MAYBELL: At least Benji tried. That should count for something.

PETE: You call that "Trying"?

SCIENTIST 3: Benji?

MAYBELL: Yes, I do!

GYNA: Benji is Benjamin.

SCIENTIST 1: Ms Marks's first victim. They had a long-term thing.

SCIENTIST 3: Oh, yeah. I keep forgetting they weren't all one-night stands—

MAYBELL: I'm sorry I haven't checked "artist" off my "Bang" list yet. Maybe I should go out and sleep with one so he can paint you a precious star map in 3-d!

SCIENTIST 2: Interesting idea…

GYNA: But artists are so moody—

PETE: Maybell isn't sexing anyone else. Artist, or no—

MAYBELL: The point is, they're making an effort, and all you're doing is bagging on them. Look at the blood coming out of their noses! And why is Jim tied up? They got in a fight and none of you care?

PETE: Of course we care. We are all here trying to save them! But, great Carl Sagan, Maybell—we can't help them if they don't take this seriously! (*He turns to back to the scientists.*) What about the satellite?

SCIENTIST 1: Nothing yet.

(*PETE sighs.*)

PETE: Weeping, weeping, William Herschel.

MAYBELL: What does that mean?

PETE: It means we need to you to send them another message.

Coitus...

(*VINCENT and JIM's kitchen. CHOW and VINCENT unpack bags from a recent shopping trip. The various items are eclectic, to say the least:*)

(*A pair of dish gloves, a giant box of trash bags, jumbo cookies, and a Mardi Gras mask sit on the table...*)

(*VINCENT pulls out a plunger with aplomb.*)

(*CHOW is unimpressed.*)

VINCENT: Okay, what's the matter?

CHOW: I just keep thinking about what Maybell said—

(*VINCENT groans.*)

VINCENT: No. Way.

CHOW: She's just trapped in that lab, like a guinea pig.

VINCENT: A guinea pig that sent my best friend to space.

CHOW: Right...but not intentionally.

VINCENT: I can't believe you still think that matters!

CHOW: I can't believe you don't!

VINCENT: I can't believe I'm here doing this with you, when you are obviously so callous—

CHOW: I am NOT callous—

VINCENT: —to think that her lack of intent erases—

CHOW: I didn't say it erases anything

VINCENT: —the fact that she is super fucking dangerous!

CHOW: They're making her send huge things to space using only her vagina!

VINCENT: Her super vagina.

CHOW: Hey—

VINCENT: Hey, what?

CHOW: I thought *my* vagina was super.

VINCENT: Your vagina is super. It's super, super.

CHOW: Mmmm.

VINCENT: And it totally does all the things it's supposed to do in a super, super way.

CHOW: I like where this is going...

VINCENT: It's so super, that I want to get all up inside it and make you super come so super hard—

CHOW: Oh my GOD, you're so hot right now!

VINCENT: Let's not fight.

CHOW: Okay.

(CHOW *and* VINCENT *kiss into black-out. Some of their items go rolling…*)

Meanwhile…in Space

(*The guys hang out, sulking, as* ELI *reads* MAYBELL'*s letter.*)

ELI: "Dear Jim, Eli, Kumail, Benji, Leon, Nikolàs and Jared (It's so great to finally know your name, by the way. They found a missing person report on you taken out by your mother. I told them to call her ASAP, but they're worried about people discovering my vagina has light-speed travel skills and freaking out, so I don't know if they'll do it.)"

JARED: That's fucked up!

ELI: Does that mean they haven't contacted any of our families?

JIM: My roommate is probably losing his shit!

NICOLÁS: Fuck the government, man!

JIM: He's ex-military—

BEN: My parents probably think I'm dead.

JIM: He won't let my disappearance go unchecked.

ELI: (*Over the din*) "So good news—the satellite didn't kill me! Yay!"

LEON: Yay.

BEN: That is good news—

NICOLÁS: Shut up, Benji.

ELI: "The scientists here are all kinds of worried about you. I am too. It looks like you've been fighting."

KUMAIL: Masters of the obvious.

ELI: "Please stop fighting with each other."

NICOLÁS: Ok, mom.

ELI: "I can't stand knowing you're all angry up there, when you're all you have."

JIM: OH MY GOD.

ELI: "NASA would like you to try another star map—can you make the stars closest to you bigger and the ones farthest away smaller?"

LEON: Nice job, Picasso.

BEN: They sent one fucking Sharpie with a fat tip!

KUMAIL: So make the big stars bigger.

BEN: Why don't you do it, Kumail?

KUMAIL: Maybe I will!

BEN: Fine!

KUMAIL: Great! Did they send more paper?

JIM: Looks like.

KUMAIL: PERFECT! *(He grabs a piece of paper and the Sharpie and starts furiously drawing.)*

ELI: "And can you try to be more specific about how you're all still alive? Also, they would like to know if there is anything you need?"

LEON: Now that's a useful question.

ELI: "And please make sure you aren't standing in front of the satellite when we take our next shot. They want to make sure it's working. Thank you. And again, I'm so very fucking sorry. Please stop fighting. Very truly yours, Maybell."

(KUMAIL makes a mess…grabs another piece of paper.)

BEN: Not so easy, is it pal?

KUMAIL: Shut up.

...Inter—

(A few days later. There are more odd items scattered around. A sweaty CHOW *sits at the table wearing the dish gloves and a sexy robe. She lights a joint.)*

*(*VINCENT *enters, similarly sweaty, and holding the plunger.)*

VINCENT: That was some serious shit.

CHOW: I know.

VINCENT: The way you—

CHOW: I know.

VINCENT: And then the way I—

CHOW: I know.

VINCENT: *(He lifts the plunger)* And then how the—

CHOW: It was perfect, babe.

*(*VINCENT *smiles, sits down with* CHOW *and takes a hit off the joint…)*

(Then he frowns.)

CHOW: What's wrong?

VINCENT: Here I am feeling so super satisfied, but then, like, all of a sudden an image of Jim getting sucked into space flew into my head and now I'm feeling guilty for being so fucking happy, right here, with you.

CHOW: Me too. But like, with Maybell instead of Jim, and she's fucking that satellite and it's ripping her apart—

VINCENT: We're a mess.

CHOW: Our minds don't want us to celebrate our love while our friends suffer.

VINCENT: Love?

CHOW: You know what I mean.

VINCENT: Shit.

CHOW: I use that word totally carelessly. You can ask Maybell, it's like, my toss-word.

(VINCENT *does not know what that means.*)

CHOW: You know, like the thing you say all the time, but don't necessarily mean in the utmost?

VINCENT: Then, you don't love me?

CHOW: I love your cock.

VINCENT: That's a part of me.

CHOW: I was being poetical.

VINCENT: My penis is pretty poetic.

CHOW: Alliteration. I like it.

VINCENT: A poetical penis and his pet pussy—

CHOW: Hey, now! I'm not anyone's "Pet"—

VINCENT: I know. I was alliterating— What's happening?

CHOW: Maybe we're moving too fast. We're trying to sex-away the pain of losing our best friends in the whole wide world and it's leading to a lot of intense feelings about penises and love and shit.

(VINCENT *kisses* CHOW.)

VINCENT: I am totally into you though.

CHOW: Yeah?

VINCENT: Yeah.

CHOW: I'm totally into you too.

(*More kissing…*)

CHOW: You *and* your cock.

VINCENT: Grab the mask!

(CHOW *grabs the mask,* VINCENT *sweeps them both up and carries them off…*)

Back in the Lab

(*The* SCIENTISTS *look tired.* GYNA *looks tired.* MAYBELL *looks more tired.*)

PETE: So tell me the bad news again? And slower this time?

SCIENTIST 1: We. Still. Haven't. Heard. From. The. Dish.

PETE: We don't know what sort of damage it may have sustained—

SCIENTIST 2: The dish looks fine.

PETE: It does?

SCIENTIST 3: From what we can see in the images from transmission four and five, yes.

(*A slide pops up of the satellite—it looks as though it has been deployed correctly.*)

SCIENTIST 1: No damage. The dish is up. Everything looks good.

PETE: And it's been how long?

SCIENTIST 1: Six days, four hours, twenty three minutes—

PETE: Shit.

SCIENTIST 3: We always knew the likelihood of satellite communication was low—

PETE: I know.

MAYBELL: Excuse me?

SCIENTIST 1: They're just too far away.

PETE: Looks like.

MAYBELL: EXCUSE ME?

PETE: Maybell, please—

MAYBELL: You made me fuck that giant metal cube even though you knew it wasn't going to work?!

SCIENTIST 1: We had to try!

MAYBELL: WE?! I don't see *you* spreading your legs for a big-ass piece of space junk—

GYNA: I'm with Maybell on this. That's pretty fucked up, even for the government.

SCIENTIST 2: It isn't junk. In all probability it is working exactly as it's supposed to. It's just going to take three or four hundred years for the signal to make it's way back to us—

MAYBELL: THREE OR FOUR HUNDRED *YEARS*?!

SCIENTIST 3: The Plaeides star cluster is four hundred and forty four light years away—

GYNA: That's where they are?

SCIENTIST 2: We don't know where they are, because none of these guys seems to be able to draw a simple star map—

PETE: We think that's the nearest star cluster, based on the visual images we've amassed so far.

MAYBELL: If this map thing is so goddamn important, then why don't you just ask them to get out of the way and take a picture of the freaking sky?

(Everyone is silent.)

SCIENTIST 1: Actually, that isn't a bad idea—

Back in Space

(JIM *reads the latest letter…*)

JIM: "…This time we'd appreciate it if you could all clear out of the way so we can take a photo of the sky. Sorry, my fault, yadda yadda, Maybell."

BEN: Guess your sky map wasn't any better than mine after all, Special K.

KUMAIL: Shut up.

JIM: They're going to come through for the picture in like, five minutes!

KUMAIL: Why didn't they just do that in the first place instead of wasting our time with these stupid drawings?

BEN: Right?

ELI: They don't seem to know what they're doing.

BEN: You know what? Fuck these guys! When is this picture getting taken?

JIM: A couple minutes—

BEN: Give me that Sharpie! (He stands up.

Back in The Lab

(*The* SCIENTISTS *look at footage from the previous communication…*)

(*All of the guys have mooned the camera. Written across their butt cheeks are letters spelling:*)

(*"Send Beer!"*)

PETE: Beer?

GYNA: Typical.

PETE: What do they think this is, a frat party?

MAYBELL: Can we send them a few bottles?

SCIENTIST 3: They can't even focus sober!

SCIENTIST 1: I think we can presume that their prolonged stint in space has perverted their mental state—

SCIENTIST 3: They've gone crazy.

PETE: We don't know that.

SCIENTIST 2: *(Looking at the image…)* But we can infer it.

PETE: Any ideas on return yet?

SCIENTIST 1: My team proposed a few things…

PETE: And?

SCIENTIST 3: They all begin with "Invent a way to travel at the speed of light."

GYNA: Ha!

MAYBELL: Maybe if we send them some beer, and something to eat, and maybe some books on astronomy, they would feel better and understand a little more what is going on—

SCIENTIST 2: Can we talk about reversing the wormhole?

PETE: How in the name of Sir Isaac H. Newton do you propose we do that?

SCIENTIST 2: Negative energy has been theorized to hold wormholes open… If we could manufacture an environment where the energy density is negative enough to match the precise moment when Ms Mark's wormhole opens, we might be able to sustain it long enough for the men to come back through—

PETE: And how are we going to create negative space of that magnitude here on Earth?

SCIENTIST 2: It's all very theoretical at the moment…

SCIENTIST 3: What about a really strong vacuum?

MAYBELL: What's that now?

SCIENTIST 1: You want to hook a vacuum up to her vagina?

MAYBELL: That doesn't sound safe—

GYNA: Because it absolutely isn't.

PETE: We might be getting into an ethical gray area here—

SCIENTIST 3: If I could just finish the hypothesis—

SCIENTIST 2: How do you propose to create a vacuum stronger than a wormhole?

SCIENTIST 3: Obviously it's just the seed of a hypothesis—

GYNA: It's ludicrous and reckless, and as the OBGYN in the room, I say NO WAY!

PETE: Mightn't it cause irreparable damage to her, er, lady area?

GYNA: Yes. Yes it would.

SCIENTIST 3: We wouldn't turn it on until the wormhole opened.

MAYBELL: Not gonna happen, you guys.

SCIENTIST 2: Has anyone thought that maybe this problem is beyond us?

SCIENTIST 3: You want to give up?

SCIENTIST 2: No—

SCIENTIST 1: Defeatist!

SCIENTIST 2: I'm an evolutionist!

SCIENTIST 3: What does Darwin have to do with this?

SCIENTIST 2: I just think "Invent the ability to travel at the speed of light" is the most practical option and an opportunity for us to evolve—

(SCIENTIST 1 *lets out a snort.*)

SCIENTIST 1: Go ahead, Scotty. And while you're at it, why don't you invent a transporter device so you can just beam them back and save us all a lot of rocket fuel in the bargain.

PETE: Doctors!

(MAYBELL *sits, feeling defeated.*)

MAYBELL: So what does this all mean?

SCIENTIST 2: It means a rescue mission is impossible.

SCIENTIST 3: And once the judge hears that, he will probably send you to work with the CIA—

GYNA: Or the FBI.

SCIENTIST 3: Out of spite.

MAYBELL: Fuck.

—uptus...

(*Different day, same story... Have these two just been sexing each other up in* VINCENT *and* JIM'S *apartment for days?*)

(*Yes. Yes they have.*)

(CHOW *and* VINCENT *are taping a series of garbage bags together and to the floor like one long garbage bag river...*)

(CHOW *has a set of swim goggles around her neck.*)

VINCENT: She really said they can't bring them back? Or just, like, reverse the black hole thing?

CHOW: It's not a black hole—

VINCENT: Space-hole—

CHOW: Worm-hole!

VINCENT: Whatever.

CHOW: No.

(Tape. Tape. Tape)

CHOW: We've got to get her out of there.

VINCENT: And unleash that vagina?

CHOW: She's not going to have sex ever again, believe me. And Maybell said that the guys are all just getting... weird in there.

VINCENT: What do you mean?

CHOW: They want beer, they don't like NASA—the last image they sent back was of them all flipping off the camera.

VINCENT: NASA won't send them beer?

CHOW: Apparently it's not in the budget.

VINCENT: But if we help her escape, we'd all be fugitives—

(CHOW and VINCENT get the final piece down. She stands up, opens a box on the table...)

CHOW: Pete's going to lose control of her in three days. The CIA, FDA, and all the other fuckin' "A"s are going to tear each other apart to get at her and start sending people and things through her vagina that they don't want here on earth. How do you think Jim's going to like his space bubble then?

VINCENT: That's fucked up.

CHOW: It's totally fucked up.

(CHOW starts pouring lube from an industrial sized jug all over the line of bags...VINCENT sheds his robe and puts on a swim-cap...)

VINCENT: If we break her out, we're going to be on the lamb together. This won't be casual sex territory anymore, you know.

CHOW: I know, baby.

(CHOW *and* VINCENT *stare into each other's eyes with intensity…*)

VINCENT: And it won't just be about Maybell. We've got to help Jim too.

CHOW: I completely agree.

VINCENT: I can't- I just can't forget he's out there, you know?

CHOW: I know. It's one of the things I find so fucking sexy about you.

VINCENT: Really?

CHOW: Yeah.

(VINCENT *heads towards the closet…*)

CHOW: What are you doing?

VINCENT: We're going to need some serious shit. I've got a lot of tactical equipment here, but we'll need to visit my storage unit too.

CHOW: I've never been so turned on in my life.

VINCENT: Yeah?

CHOW: Say it again.

VINCENT: Tactical equipment?

CHOW: Yes.

VINCENT: Tac-tical. E-quip-ment

CHOW: Oh my god!

(CHOW *puts the goggles on and takes a step towards* VINCENT; *he braces himself at the far end of the bags…*)

VINCENT: How're your ovaries now?

CHOW: Throbbing!

(CHOW *throws herself onto the sex slip-and-slide and goes gliding into a very ready* VINCENT. *The pair slide off stage real hot and heavy like...)*

(Black)

I'll See You in Court! Again.

(JUDGE JENKINS *and all the previous courtroom players are present except the DA.)*

(MAYBELL *sits, bummed out beyond belief.)*

(PETE *looks sweaty and anxious.)*

(GYNA, CHOW, *and* VINCENT *are also present.)*

JUDGE JENKINS: Where's the, my new—

(THE CLERK hands JUDGE JENKINS *a gavel.)*

JUDGE JENKINS: Mine had a gold band—

THE CLERK: This one came with free shipping.

JUDGE JENKINS: *(Sighs)* Go ahead.

THE CLERK: All rise! The court is now in session. The Honorable Judge Jon Jenkins presiding. The matter of the United States v. Maybell Marks, and her vagina, will now be heard.

JUDGE JENKINS: You may be seated.

MAXINE SHARP: Your Honor—

JUDGE JENKINS: Don't bother.

MAXINE SHARP: Sir?

JUDGE JENKINS: You're going to ask me to release your client from custody because the boys at NASA can't figure out a way to bring those seven fine Americans home—

US ATTORNEY EICHMAN: Six.

JUDGE JENKINS: Jumpin' Jehosephat, did one of them die?

US ATTORNEY EICHMAN: No, your honor, it's just that only six of the men are American citizens. Nicolas Ovalles is Venezuelan—

JUDGE JENKINS: Oh, okay then. So, NASA has failed their country, and a family in Venezuala.

US ATTORNEY EICHMAN: His family lives in the States.

JUDGE JENKINS: Legally?

US ATTORNEY EICHMAN: No.

JUDGE JENKINS: Does ICE know that?

US ATTORNEY EICHMAN: Er, yes. We've shared that information—

MAYBELL: Why the hell would you do that?!

JUDGE JENKINS: Bless your bleeding heart, are you a liberal?

MAYBELL: I'm a fucking human being with a beating fucking heart—

JUDGE JENKINS: Language!

MAXINE SHARP: Your honor, I fail to see how any of this is relevant—

JUDGE JENKINS: Your client is keeping real live men captive through the use of her private parts—

GYNA: Hear we go again.

JUDGE JENKINS: A problem even the idiots in the white coats can't seem to solve—

PETE: It's only been a few weeks, your honor! We can't possibly be expected to have a working solution in just two weeks!

JUDGE JENKINS: Apollo 13.

PETE: Excuse me?

JUDGE JENKINS: I saw that movie. You guys trouble-shooted a way to bring those boys home in a matter of hours.

CHOW: Trouble-*shooted*?

PETE: Those guys were just on their way to the moon—

JUDGE JENKINS: Now you're all just a bunch of theorists with your hands up in the air—

PETE: Well, perhaps if the government hadn't neutered our funding, we'd be in a better position to "trouble-shoot" this whole situation—

JUDGE JENKINS: So file a complaint with Uncle Sam! In the meantime, you're letting six fine American men, and a, what was he?

US ATTORNEY EICHMAN: Venezuelan—

JUDGE JENKINS: Right. They're rotting out there, on account of you!

US ATTORNEY EICHMAN: Your honor, with all due respect, it's obvious from Mr Sellis's report that the technology needed to return these gentlemen won't exist for eons, if ever.

PETE: Breakthroughs happen all the time—

US ATTORNEY EICHMAN: It's time we talk about how we use Ms Marks' abilities to make a better world possible here on Earth. Now.

MAYBELL: So now my pussy's some kind of "gift" to mankind?

JUDGE JENKINS: Ms Marks, I'm warning you! Say the word "pussy" one more time and I'll have you put in a holding cell—

MAYBELL: Put me in a holding cell, and I'll masturbate a wormhole so big, it'll suck this whole courthouse into space!

(The room erupts.)

JUDGE JENKINS: Order! Order! ORDER!

(No one feels like falling into order…)

JUDGE JENKINS: *(To* PETE*)* Can she do that?

PETE: No.

JUDGE JENKINS: *(To the room)* She can't do that!

PETE: At least, we don't *think* she can do that.

(They erupt again.)

JUDGE JENKINS: What's that now?

PETE: Well, this is why we need more time with her—

US ATTORNEY EICHMAN: With all due respect—

PETE: Holy Isaac Asimov, you can quit it with the "Respect" malarkey—

US ATTORNEY EICHMAN: With all due *respect*, the CIA and the FBI, in a rare show of solidarity, have expressed a willingness to allow continued scientific study of Ms Marks, if NASA will help us put her wormhole to use in clearing a few unsavory individuals off the most wanted list—

CHOW: *(A sharp intake of breath)* Sex Assassin!

MAYBELL: I don't want to sleep with criminals—

AGENT BUNCH: You'd be providing an invaluable service.

MAYBELL: I'm not a prostitute.

AGENT X: We absolutely would not call you that.

MAYBELL: I have to come. You know? For the wormhole to work? I can't come on command. I can't orgasm on Kim Jong Un's balls—

(JUDGE JENKINS *gavels hard.*)

MAXINE SHARP: Is the court honestly saying that my client should prostitute herself for Uncle Sam?

AGENT BUNCH: It wouldn't be the first time someone—

EPA CHIEF: Chief Jolly, your honor. EPA. We think that Ms Marks', ah, special talent, opens a lot of doors for dealing with the nation's toxic waste problems—

MAYBELL: No one is shooting toxic waste up my whoopsie-doodle!

PETE: Doing so would definitely kill the men on the other side.

EPA CHIEF: What are you talking about? It's space. There's plenty of room!

PETE: Well, that's the funny thing. The men seem to be trapped in a bubble of sorts. They are completely safe, un-aged, and healthy, even though they haven't had food or water in years. Toxic sludge would fill that bubble—they'd have nowhere to hide.

JUDGE JENKINS: Are you saying Ms Marks' vagina is some sort of fountain of youth?

PETE: Er, no. *You're* saying that. But it's technically true. You just have to be willing to trade having a life here on earth in order to live forever in Ms Marks' vagina—

MAXINE SHARP: We are getting wildly off topic—

JUDGE JENKINS: I agree. Obviously no one would want to live forever in a space bubble if they can't take advantage of the benefits that eternal youth would inspire—

US ATTORNEY EICHMAN: I move that we remand Ms Marks to federal custody immediately.

JUDGE JENKINS: —unless we all went through Ms Marks' vagina and rebuilt a society of eternal youth on the other side, hahahaha.

(AGENT BUNCH *and* AGENT X *give each other a look.*)

JUDGE JENKINS: In any case—

MAXINE SHARP: I have to strenuously object to your honor's behavior—

JUDGE JENKINS: Object away.

MAXINE SHARP: My client has rights—

(*But* JUDGE JENKINS *waves her off…*)

JUDGE JENKINS: Had. Had rights. She's a threat to national security, she's a man-napper, and we can probably add terrorism to her growing list of charges—

MAXINE SHARP: What?

JUDGE JENKINS: Not giving those boys back is terrifying! Terrifying!

AGENT X: Do we know, is this bit of space a new, well, could we call it a new "territory" of sorts?

US ATTORNEY EICHMAN: Effective occupation laws would certainly seem to apply—

AGENT BUNCH: There is the issue of the Venezuelan…

US ATTORNEY EICHMAN: So one seventh of the territory is contested. Whose gonna' win?

JUDGE JENKINS: A new American territory. The new "Old West". And the FBI wants to populate it with outlaws—

AGENT X: Some of our proposed targets have considerable assets that could prove useful in establishing a colony—

MAYBELL: Now you want to colonize my vagina?

JUDGE JENKINS: With a few important elements, you could really turn it into something—

PETE: You're talking about terraforming, which is a highly theoretical science fiction device—

JUDGE JENKINS: Well what do you propose we do, Mr Sellis? From what I read in your report, these boys just want to come home. But you're saying you can't make that happen, so why can't we send some home to them?

PETE: Marie Curie's knapsack! The logical fallacies you use to arrive at not only impractical, but delusional solutions, is mind-numbing—

EPA CHIEF: The EPA has some questionably sourced sand we've been trying to get rid of—

MAYBELL: No one is sending anything else up my freaking' poke-hole!!!!

(JUDGE JENKINS *picks up his gavel…*)

MAYBELL: These guys, all of them, American or not, are alive out there, floating in impossible space! At first, when I found out what had happened, I wanted to die. I thought, maybe if I die, they'll all come back—

JUDGE JENKINS: Is that possible?

PETE: Most likely no. The wormhole will either just collapse or cease to function—

JUDGE JENKINS: Shame.

MAYBELL: But now, now I am like, so a hundred percent sure that regardless of what any of this batshit crazy shit means, it's my responsibility to make sure you numskulls don't ruin it. So, you are NOT going to send anyone else up my vagina, global terrorists or no. And YOU, you sick fuck, are not going to use my vagina as some sort of old-west diorama. These men, inside my wormhole, are breathing, speaking, living human beings and I'm going to protect them from all of you if it's the last thing I do.

JUDGE JENKINS: Not the most moving speech, but—

(MAYBELL *flips a switch, and we hear a gentle buzz…*)

JUDGE JENKINS: What is that?

GYNA: If I'm not mistaken, it's the Vib-o-matic, seven thousand.

MAYBELL: Eight thousand.

GYNA: Nice choice!

MAYBELL: Thank you.

JUDGE JENKINS: What in the name of all that's holy is a Vib-o—

MAYBELL: It's a vibrator, Judge Jenkins. And it's in my pants.

JUDGE JENKINS: Oh my God.

MAYBELL: Right next to my clitoris, pressing the doorbell to the Big O.

JUDGE JENKINS: Bailiff!

MAYBELL: The biggest O that ever O-ed.

PETE: She's going to suck us all out into space!

US ATTORNEY EICHMAN: I thought you said she couldn't do that!

PETE: That's what I've been trying to tell you! We don't know *what* she can and can't do, we've only been studying her for a few fucking weeks!

GYNA: If ever a vibrator could make a woman climax a building into space, the Vib-O-Matic Eight Thousand is it.

(MAYBELL *moans…*)

US ATTORNEY EICHMAN: Somebody shoot her!

PETE: No! Once the anomaly is engaged, a sudden change in its bio-pressure could create a negative reaction powerful enough to unravel the gravitational force anchoring it to Ms Marks' vagina, unleashing it on this courtroom and possibly destabilizing our very universe!

AGENT BUNCH: Use English!

PETE: If you shoot her now, the wormhole could suck us all through, every man, woman, and child on planet earth. Plus Earth itself. And maybe even some microbes from Mars. The entire solar system would be in jeopardy! It would be like a, like a, ah…a big, the biggest, like, just—*BANG!*

(MAYBELL *moans…*)

JUDGE JENKINS: Okay, okay. No toxic waste.

MAYBELL: And no criminals!

JUDGE JENKINS: That too.

MAYBELL: I want control over my own vagina!

JUDGE JENKINS: Okay, okay, anything you want. Just stop before you kill us all.

(But MAYBELL *is vibing out…*)

MAYBELL: You're lying. You won't let me go. You're all liars!

PETE: Maybell?

MAYBELL: I can't stop it—

PETE: Please, Maybell—

MAYBELL: I don't *want* to stop it!

JUDGE JENKINS: Everyone get out! Get out now!

MAYBELL: Can't stop, won't stop, can't stop, won't stop… Oh, oh, oh- You can run, but you can't hide, motherfuckers!

(Everyone runs out of the courtroom.)

(Except PETE, GYNA, CHOW, *and* VINCENT…*)*

*(*MAYBELL *climaxes in operatic fashion…)*

MAYBELL: TOMMY LEE JONES ON ROLLER SKATES! *(Then she slumps over, nearly unconscious.)*

*(*VINCENT *wastes no time getting a harnass on her… well, he wastes a little time. He's a little nervous about getting too close and maybe sucked into outer space.)*

CHOW: Maybell?

MAYBELL: Oh my God…

GYNA: Holy shit, it worked.

PETE: That was some good acting—

MAYBELL: Who said I was acting?

PETE: You actually climaxed? Here? In an uncontrolled environment?

MAYBELL: Yes, grandpa! Calm down.

PETE: You could have sucked us all into space!

MAYBELL: But I didn't.

VINCENT: I estimate we've got two-point-five minutes before they bring in SWAT—

*(*MAYBELL *hugs* CHOW.*)*

MAYBELL: *(Overlapping)* You guys are incredible!

CHOW: And maybe thirty seconds before she passes out cold. Maybell?

MAYBELL: *(Totally falling asleep)* I'm awake. I'm getting better at managing my super powers…

*(*CHOW *helps* VINCENT *with* MAYBELL*'s harness.)*

CHOW: I can't believe Tommy Lee Jones is your masturbation animal.

GYNA: Where's my Vib-O-Matic?

MAYBELL: Probably landing at the feet of a very confused dude I once banged.

GYNA: Maybell, that was a sample item!

MAYBELL: So tell them it was out of this world.

GYNA: I was going to try it out with this great bottle of Pinot Noir—

VINCENT: We're losing precious escape seconds here, people! Harness check!

(Everyone peels off a layer, revealing matching harnesses with a "Check!")

MAYBELL: Where are we going?

VINCENT: Turns out I know a guy.

CHOW: He's a science guy.

GYNA: With lots of money.

PETE: So much money. And fame. Lots and lots of fame.

CHOW: He lives far away from government oversight committees and EPA dickbags.

PETE: We will, of course, continue to do research—

CHOW: But you won't be trapped!

PETE: NASA will be working this completely off the books.

VINCENT: I should tell you now, I'm only doing this because Chow said we could send Jim some of his things.

MAYBELL: Sure, sure, I can do that. This baby's a lot more powerful under the hood than she realized!

(A chopper is heard overhead.)

VINCENT: That's our ride. He's only touching down for nintey seconds! MOVE, PEOPLE!

(They all go running...)

PETE: Neil deGrasse Tyson, protect us!

Six-Packs and Underoos

(The dudes look dejected.)

(Suddenly JARED *gets hit in the face with a giant jiggly dildo:)*

JARED: Ow, shit. *(He jumps up:)* Delivery!

(The guys stand to attention...)

(The dildo is followed by a paper airplane...which has a string connecting it to a series of other strung-together items:)

(Body pillow, David Bowie T-shirt, packages of: socks, underwear, shorts, T-shirts, an ipod, ipod speaker, new deck of cards, poker chips, Monopoly, Risk, Cards Against Humanity, a large white-board, a package of whiteboard markers, some books, some magazines, an ipad, a pocket projector, and finally, some mother-fucking beer! A long line of individual beer bottles tied to one another.)

(It's a beautiful and strange sight. The items will take a little while to all float on...)

KUMAIL: Grab the— Holy shit! Get the airplane!

JIM: Bowie! *(He grabs the shirt, holds it close and immediately puts it on.)*

(The men lunge at the underwear like, well, like men who have been mostly naked and dressed in tampons for a very long time.)

ELI: Dibs!

NICOLÁS: Hallelujah!

LEON: What size are the skivvies?

JARED: Looks like a mix.

BEN: Don't even try to say you need more room than the rest of us—

LEON: I'm sorry, I wasn't nineteen when I banged my way to space, Skeletor!

BEN: Skeletor was seriously ripped.

JIM: Hey, that's my pillow!

ELI: Why isn't there anything of mine in here?

JARED: Is that Monopoly?

NICOLÁS: Dibs on the red shirt.

LEON: Dude.

NICOLÁS: What? I look good in red.

KUMAIL: Guys, listen to this! *(He reads a letter from MAYBELL.)* "Dear Space Dudes, as you can probably tell, I have busted out of government custody and am finally calling the shots on my super vagina. I'm still working with NASA, but in an off-the-books manner. They don't like it much, but it was better than losing me to the government whack-jobs who want to use me for mal-intent."

BEN: What does that mean?

KUMAIL: Who knows.
"I'm now free to send you beer, music, and other small things on occasion."

ELI: Did she say beer?

KUMAIL: "Jim, please know your roommate has requested I send your favorite David Bowie shirt and body pillow. He was adamant about the pillow." *(He looks up.)*

KUMAIL: What's so special about the pillow, dude?

JIM: I've had it forever.

NICOLÁS: Girlfriend substitute.

JIM: No—

JARED: *(To* NICOLÁS*)* I believe that!

JIM: It's memory foam and I've put a lot of time into getting the indents just right, okay?

BEN: Guys, leave him alone about the pillow. I want to hear more from Maybell.

NICOLÁS: Of course you do, Benji.

BEN: Shut up.

*(*LEON *jumps…he's spied the beer!)*

LEON: Guys! Am I hallucinating?

JIM: Now we're talking!

JARED: There is a God!

KUMAIL: More like a Goddess.

JARED: And her name is Maybell!

JIM: Oh, come on—

KUMAIL: No, think about it. We're totally at the mercy of what happens to her back on Earth. If that's not a diety-type relationship, I don't know what is.

ELI: That's a stretch dude.

JIM: Yeah. Major stretch. Is it all domestic?

NICOLÁS: I see a few craft beers, some IPAs and, looks like a can of- Busch.

KUMAIL: A twisted deity.

JIM: If anything, she's like, our mom, dude. Not a Goddess.

LEON: I have to agree with Jim on that one. Besides, we all know she's human. We banged her.

ELI: Yeah we did.

(They high five.)

BEN: And wound up in a scientifically impossible space bubble where none of us ever age. Yeah, sounds real "human" and not at all goddess-like to me.

JARED: Shit.

LEON: I hadn't thought of it like that.

JIM: So what's the deal with the whiteboard? Are we supposed to play Pictionary?

JARED: I love that game!

NICOLÁS: I call NOT being on Kumail's team.

KUMAIL: Dude, I don't know what a freaking star map is supposed to look like!

NICOLÁS: Uh-huh.

(KUMAIL reads some more.)

KUMAIL: Whatever. Here:
"The whiteboard and markers are to help cut down on paper waste while you continue to communicate with your home planet, because Pete, our NASA man here, still has plenty of questions."

ELI: *(Eye-roll)* Great.

KUMAIL: "And you're going to have plenty of time to answer them, because since my vagina uses exotic matter, or some other kind of super negative energy force never before seen on Earth, to open and close the wormhole that sucked you all out into Space, you're far as fuck from planet Earth, and stuck there to boot."

BEN: Shit.

NICOLÁS: We're not going home?

LEON: Shit, shit.

KUMAIL: According to Maybell, they have to invent the ability to travel at light-speed first.

JARED: Shit, shit, shit!

KUMAIL: Looks like Ellen is a no-go, NICOLÁS.

JARED: *(Sincerely)* Sorry about that, man.

BEN: *(Also totally sincere)* Yeah. We wanted that to happen for you, dude.

JIM: Yeah.

NICOLÁS: *(Emotionally)* Thanks.

(The guys share an awkward, but sweet, moment of shared sympathy.)

ELI: So they're just giving up?

KUMAIL: No, looks like the they want to invent light-speed travel. HA! That's insane. They're all living on some billionaire tech dude's private island trying to figure it all out. Listen to this:
"Basically we've all sequestered ourselves away from the government in order to keep working on a way to make this sci-fi fantasy real. We are all seriously dedicated to cracking open the mysteries of my vagina so that you can one day come home."

LEON: That's good, they're not giving up.

JIM: Yeah.

NICOLÁS: Yeah. Shit.

(ELI lifts his beer in a toast.)

ELI: To not giving up!

(Everyone responds with a "Hear hear!" And "To not giving up" and "I'll drink to that!" and "Fuck yeah!")

KUMAIL: "Anyway, that's a lot of heavy shit to digest—"

NICOLÁS: No shit.

KUMAIL: "—which is why I sent through a few cases of beer. I have no idea if it will still be cold, but trust that it was cold when I sent it through. Cold as fuck. And I slid it through my vagina in order to send it to you. I also sent some music, which Pete theorizes you will be able to listen to forever, since you all seem to be subsisting on some kind of super energy field thing. He thinks the same force will keep the iPod charged indefinitely. But he wants you to give him reports on the battery life so he can confirm.

Umm, that's about it. I'm basically a nun now, so you don't have to worry about any more men showing up over there. Maybe a few more vibrators, but not any more men, LOL.

I also want to tell you that although I didn't know all of you very well, I care about you all a great deal. I will do everything I can to keep you safe out there. Good luck, kick back, and enjoy the eternal youth, fellas!"

(Beat)

(Beat)

NICOLÁS: I always dreamed of being an astronaut.

KUMAIL: I'll toast to that.

JARED: Who feels like cracking into Risk?

LEON: I haven't played that game in ages!

KUMAIL: Dude, none of us have.

BEN: I'm down.

ELI: Me too.

JIM: Me three.

NICOLÁS: I'll play

KUMAIL: Why not?

JARED: Not the table!

(The others repeat "Not the table", with LEON *the last one to chime in.)*

LEON: Shit.

KUMAIL: We'll ask her to send a card table or something next time, man.

LEON: Yeah, okay.

JIM: Dibs on red!

ELI: Dude, I'm always red.

JARED: Blue!

KUMAIL: Guys—

BEN: We didn't open it up for dibs yet.

JARED: Dibs is dibs.

LEON: I want to be red.

BEN: You're the table.

JIM: You want a little cheese with that whine?

LEON: Shut up.

KUMAIL: Somebody pass me another beer.

(Lights fade on the dudes as they continue acting like… dudes trapped in impossible space.)

Sex on the beach

*(*MAYBELL *reclines on a beach chair.)*

*(*CHOW *reclines next to her.)*

CHOW: Now this is the motherfucking LIFE!

MAYBELL: Word.

*(*MAYBELL *and* CHOW *sit, relaxed for a moment…)*

CHOW: Too bad we couldn't bring your bong on the plane—

MAYBELL: I thought you were giving up weed for these magical Vincent babies you keep talking about.

CHOW: You know I'm just using that as a euphemism for being in heat. The man makes me crazy. I mean, look at him! Look at his back. He's out there swimming in the huge ass ocean, and he still looks like he's totally in charge.

(A beat while they admire VINCENT...*)*

CHOW: I'm sorry. I should up shut about him. Do you miss Jim?

MAYBELL: Oh, God, no! I barely knew him. And he was kind of a, well, don't tell Vincent this, but just not my type at all. He was totally freaked out that I had a cat.

CHOW: The best cat in the whole fucking world!

MAYBELL: I know!

CHOW: That little angel didn't cry the whole time you had him in your carry-on!

MAYBELL: I know. I fucking love him.

CHOW: Totally.

(Beat)

MAYBELL: I do miss being normal though.

CHOW: Oh, fuck, yeah—no, I get that.

MAYBELL: And I, well—I feel kind of like, a lot of responsibility now, you know?

CHOW: It's like you have invisible children, or something.

MAYBELL: Exactly! That is exactly it.

CHOW: They need you. They're your man-babies. On a, like, a worm-hole umbilical cord...

MAYBELL: That's some deep ass poetry, Chow.

CHOW: Word.

(Beat)

MAYBELL: Direction change.

CHOW: Do it.

MAYBELL: Do you believe in religion?

CHOW: Religion is a bunch of shit some dudes from, like, forever ago, made up to control the world.

MAYBELL: Hm…

CHOW: God, on the other hand…well, I've been too high too many times not to believe in Shim. Hey, your magic vagina isn't making you get all religious here, is it? Because I am NOT the person to talk to about that shit—

MAYBELL: No. I'm just, Pete said something—I'm sure it's stupid as fuck -but I haven't been able to, like, forget about it—

CHOW: So spill.

MAYBELL: Well, he said that, he has this crazy theory that maybe when I die—

CHOW: Shut up.

MAYBELL: Just listen—

CHOW: You're not dying, for like, ever!

MAYBELL: Yeah, but when I'm super old and brittle as fuck, and I fall down a cliff and die because my bones all shatter—

CHOW: Jesus—

MAYBELL: Shut up. When that happens, he thinks that everything down below will destabilize and the entire universe will get sucked through my wormhole. He keeps calling it the Big Bang Part 2.

CHOW: My brain needs to be in an altered state for this level of conversation.

MAYBELL: I know, it's deep.

CHOW: Too deep.

MAYBELL: Yeah.

CHOW: So, you're the Big Bang?

MAYBELL: Well, maybe. I mean, he was using all this crazy science-speak that sounded super legit. He said something about time being circular, and deja vu maybe not being "quack science" after all—and that basically, I might be the Alpha and the Omega of everything, and life as we know it may all be about to end and also reborn, through my vagina, in an entirely new universe.

CHOW: Fuuuuuck.

MAYBELL: Yeah.

(CHOW *considers this new theory…*)

CHOW: If we all go through your vagina when you die, I'd better be first.

MAYBELL: Okay.

CHOW: I'm serious! You're my best friend and my soul's mate, girl! I need to be at the front of that line!

(MAYBELL *sticks out her pinky, and* MAYBELL *and* CHOW *pinky swear…*)

MAYBELL: Deal.

CHOW: Solid.

(*A handsome man approaches… He's a* BUTLER.)

BUTLER: Can I get you anything else, Ms Marks?

MAYBELL: How about Sex on the Beach.

CHOW: HA, yeah right, and then make yourself an Adios Mother Fucker!

(MAYBELL *and* CHOW *cackle.*)

MAYBELL: Both. Can we have both?

BUTLER: Of course. I'll just consult the bartending recipe book Ms Li so thoughtfully purchased for me.

MAYBELL: Thank you.

BUTLER: Mr Musk has asked that I remind you about the three o'clock radiation experiment.

CHOW: Radiation?

BUTLER: He's also asked that I remind you to wear your sunscreen—

MAYBELL: Shit, okay.

BUTLER: And Mr Sellis has asked that you please finish filling out the questionnaire he gave you.

MAYBELL: Got it. Thank you.

(The BUTLER *gives* MAYBELL *a look…)*

MAYBELL: I said I got it! Sheesh.

CHOW: Dude, nanny much?

(The BUTLER *turns to leave…)*

CHOW: Don't forget the drinks! *(To* MAYBELL*)* What's the radiation experiment?

MAYBELL: They want me to masturbate with some radiation sort of divining tool that will give them a bunch of math when I orgasm.

CHOW: Oh my God. You sure you're okay with all this?

MAYBELL: Yes. I am. Really. I mean, I'm not sure what to do with the whole Big Bang theory thing, and I'll never have legit sex again, but maybe I'm a Goddess with cult-fame on the horizon, so, that's kind of like, the tits!

CHOW: The. Motherfucking. Tits. Does that make me your acolyte?

MAYBELL: Yes. Yes, it does. Which means you have to help me with this long-ass questionnaire.

(Handing CHOW *a small, but thick, bundle of papers:)*

MAYBELL: It's boring as shit.

CHOW: How many questions are there?

MAYBELL: I don't know. A thousand?

CHOW: Good thing we have the afternoon sun to keep us on track.

MAYBELL: And a butler.

CHOW: And boozy drinks on their way…

MAYBELL: Damn skippy.

CHOW: Alright, Madame Bang, first question…

END OF PLAY

www.ingramcontent.com/pod-product-compliance
Lightning Source LLC
Chambersburg PA
CBHW052110090426
42741CB00009B/1755